P9-APL-320

To:

_____

From:

_____

The LORD is faithful to all his promises
and loving toward all he has made.

Psalm 145:13

Promises for Dads from the New International Version
Copyright 2001 by Zondervan
ISBN 0-310-98265-0

All Scripture quotations, unless otherwise noted, are taken from the *Holy Bible: New International Version.*®
Copyright 1973, 1978, 1984, by International Bible Society. Used by permission of Zondervan. All rights reserved.

The "NIV" and "New International Version" trademarks are registered in the United States Patent and Trademark Office by International Bible Society. Use of either trademark requires the permission of International Bible Society.

All rights reserved. No part of this publication may be reproduced, stored in a retrieval system, or transmitted in any form or by any means—electronic, mechanical, photocopy, recording, or any other—except for brief quotations in printed reviews, without the prior permission of the publisher.

Requests for information should be addressed to:

Inspirio, The gift group of Zondervan
Grand Rapids, Michigan 49530
http://www.inspiriogifts.com

Associate Editor: Molly C. Detweiler
Compiler: Robin S. Schmitt
Cover Designer: David Carlson
Design Manager: Amy E. Langeler
Interior design: Todd Sprague

Printed in the United States of America

02 03 04/RRD/ 3 2 1

PROMISES
for
DADS

from the
New International Version

inspirio™

CONTENTS

BLESSINGS

Blessed are all who fear the LORD,
   who walk in his ways.
You will eat the fruit of your labor;
   blessings and prosperity will be yours.
Your wife will be like a fruitful vine
   within your house;
your sons will be like olive shoots
   around your table.
Thus is the man blessed
   who fears the LORD.

Psalm 128:1–4

Every good and perfect gift is from above, coming
down from the Father of the heavenly lights, who
does not change like shifting shadows.

James 1:17

Blessed is the man
   who makes the LORD his trust.

Psalm 40:4

BLESSINGS

This is what the LORD says—
I will pour out my Spirit on your offspring,
  and my blessing on your descendants.
They will spring up like grass in a meadow,
  like poplar trees by flowing streams.

Isaiah 44:2–4

Taste and see that the LORD is good;
  blessed is the man who takes refuge in him.

Psalm 34:8

You anoint my head with oil, O LORD;
  my cup overflows.
Surely goodness and love will follow me
  all the days of my life,
and I will dwell in the house of the LORD
  forever.

Psalm 23:5–6

BLESSINGS

Blessed are those who have learned to acclaim you,
who walk in the light of your presence,
O LORD.

Psalm 89:15

From the fullness of God's grace we have all
received one blessing after another.

John 1:16

A generous man will himself be blessed.

Proverbs 22:9

Delight yourself in the LORD
and he will give you the desires of your heart.

Psalm 37:4

Blessed are those who hunger
and thirst for righteousness,
for they will be filled.

Matthew 5:6

BLESSINGS

How great is your goodness, O LORD,
  which you have stored up for those who
        fear you,
which you bestow in the sight of men
  on those who take refuge in you.

Psalm 31:19

A faithful man will be richly blessed.

Proverbs 28:20

God will bless us,
  and all the ends of the earth will fear him.

Psalm 67:7

The LORD gives strength to his people;
  the LORD blesses his people with peace.

Psalm 29:11

BLESSINGS

Praise be to the God and Father of our Lord Jesus
Christ, who has blessed us in the heavenly realms
with every spiritual blessing in Christ.

Ephesians 1:3

Blessed is the man who fears the LORD,
   who finds great delight in his commands.
His children will be mighty in the land;
   the generation of the upright will be blessed.

Psalm 112:1–2

Blessed are the people whose God is the LORD.

Psalm 144:15

Surely, O LORD, you bless the righteous;
   you surround them with your favor as with
      a shield.

Psalm 5:12

BLESSINGS

The LORD blesses the home of the righteous.

Proverbs 3:33

The righteous man leads a blameless life;
    blessed are his children after him.

Proverbs 20:7

The LORD longs to be gracious to you;
    he rises to show you compassion.
For the LORD is a God of justice.
    Blessed are all who wait for him!

Isaiah 30:18

"My people will be filled with my bounty,"
    declares the LORD.

Jeremiah 31:14

The Lord richly blesses all who call on him.

Romans 10:12

BLESSINGS

Blessed is the man who trusts in the LORD,
   whose confidence is in him.
He will be like a tree planted by the water
   that sends out its roots by the stream.
It does not fear when heat comes;
   its leaves are always green.
It has no worries in a year of drought
   and never fails to bear fruit.

Jeremiah 17:7–8

The LORD bless you
   and keep you;
the LORD make his face shine upon you
   and be gracious to you;
the LORD turn his face toward you
   and give you peace.

Numbers 6:24–26

Reflections on
BLESSINGS

_____

_____

_____

_____

_____

_____

_____

_____

_____

_____

_____

_____

_____

_____

_____

_____

_____

CHILDREN

Sons are a heritage from the LORD,
   children a reward from him.
Like arrows in the hands of a warrior
   are sons born in one's youth.
Blessed is the man
   whose quiver is full of them.

Psalm 127:3–5

All your sons will be taught by the LORD,
   and great will be your children's peace.

Isaiah 54:13

Has not the LORD made [the husband and wife]
one? In flesh and spirit they are his. And why one?
Because he was seeking godly offspring.

Malachi 2:15

A wise son brings joy to his father.

Proverbs 10:1

CHILDREN

Jesus said, "Let the little children come to me, and do not hinder them, for the kingdom of God belongs to such as these." ... And he took the children in his arms, put his hands on them and blessed them.

Mark 10:14, 16

O LORD, our Lord,
     how majestic is your name in all the earth!
You have set your glory
     above the heavens.
From the lips of children and infants
     you have ordained praise.

Psalm 8:1–2

Jesus said, "If anyone gives even a cup of cold water to one of these little ones because he is my disciple, I tell you the truth, he will certainly not lose his reward."

Matthew 10:42

CHILDREN

Train a child in the way he should go,
and when he is old he will not turn from it.

Proverbs 22:6

Discipline your son, and he will give you peace;
he will bring delight to your soul.

Proverbs 29:17

Jesus said, "Whoever welcomes one of these little
children in my name welcomes me; and whoever
welcomes me does not welcome me but the one
who sent me."

Mark 9:37

CHILDREN

The father of a righteous man has great joy;
    he who has a wise son delights in him.

Proverbs 23:24

May the LORD bless you from Zion
    all the days of your life;
may you see the prosperity of Jerusalem,
    and may you live to see your
       children's children.

Psalm 128:5–6

Reflections on
CHILDREN

_____

_____

_____

_____

_____

_____

_____

_____

_____

_____

_____

_____

_____

_____

COMFORT

Praise be to God and Father of our Lord Jesus
Christ, the Father of compassion and the God of
all comfort, who comforts us in all our troubles,
so that we can comfort those in any trouble with
the comfort we ourselves have received from God.

2 Corinthians 1:3–4

Blessed are those who mourn,
   for they will be comforted.

Matthew 5:4

You are the God who sees me.

Genesis 16:13

Cast all your anxiety on God because he cares
for you.

1 Peter 5:7

COMFORT

The LORD is my shepherd, I shall not be in want.
  He makes me lie down in green pastures,
he leads me beside quiet waters,
  he restores my soul.
He guides me in paths of righteousness
  for his name's sake.
Even though I walk
  through the valley of the shadow of death,
I will fear no evil,
  for you are with me;
your rod and your staff,
  they comfort me.

Psalm 23:1–4

COMFORT

The LORD is close to the brokenhearted
    and saves those who are crushed in spirit.

Psalm 34:18

Come near to God and he will come near to you.

James 4:8

Your righteousness reaches to the skies, O God,
    you who have done great things.
    Who, O God, is like you? . . .
    You will restore my life again;
from the depths of the earth
    you will again bring me up.
You will increase my honor
    and comfort me once again.

Psalm 71:19–21

COMFORT

O LORD, my comfort in my suffering is this:
　　Your promise preserves my life.

Psalm 119:50

Shout for joy, O heavens;
　　rejoice, O earth;
　　burst into song, O mountains!
For the LORD comforts his people
　　and will have compassion on his afflicted ones.

Isaiah 49:13

"I will turn their mourning into gladness;
　　I will give them comfort and joy instead
　　　　of sorrow,"
　　declares the LORD.

Jeremiah 31:13

COMFORT

Through Christ our comfort overflows.

2 Corinthians 1:5

"I, even I, am he who comforts you,"
    declares the LORD.

Isaiah 51:12

We dealt with each of you as a father deals with
his own children, encouraging, comforting and
urging you to live lives worthy of God, who calls
you into his kingdom and glory.

1 Thessalonians 2:11–12

When I said, "My foot is slipping,"
    your love, O LORD, supported me.
When anxiety was great within me,
    your consolation brought joy to my soul.

Psalm 94:18–19

COMFORT

Have faith in the LORD your God and you will
be upheld.

2 Chronicles 20:20

You understand, O LORD;
remember me and care for me.

Jeremiah 15:15

You, O LORD, have helped me and comforted me.

Psalm 86:17

**May your unfailing love be my comfort,
O LORD,
according to your promise to your servant.**

Psalm 119:76

Reflections on
COMFORT

_____

_____

_____

_____

_____

_____

_____

_____

_____

_____

_____

_____

_____

_____

_____

_____

_____

_____

COURAGE

Be strong and courageous. Do not be terrified; do
not be discouraged, for the LORD your God will
be with you wherever you go.

Joshua 1:9

God did not give us a spirit of timidity, but a
spirit of power, of love and of self-discipline.

2 Timothy 1:7

Be still, and know that I am God.

Psalm 46:10

"Do not fear, for I am with you;
    do not be dismayed, for I am your God.
I will strengthen you and help you;
    I will uphold you with my righteous
        right hand,"
        declares the LORD.

Isaiah 41:10

COURAGE

Jesus said, "Do not be afraid, little flock, for your
Father has been pleased to give you the kingdom."

Luke 12:32

The LORD is my light and my salvation—
   whom shall I fear?
The LORD is the stronghold of my life—
   of whom shall I be afraid?

Psalm 27:1

You did not receive a spirit that makes you a slave
again to fear, but you received the Spirit of
sonship. And by him we cry, *"Abba,* Father."

Romans 8:15

Jesus said, "Peace I leave with you; my peace I
give you. I do not give to you as the world gives.
Do not let your hearts be troubled and do not
be afraid."

John 14:27

COURAGE

A righteous man will have no fear of bad news;
   his heart is steadfast, trusting in the LORD.
His heart is secure, he will have no fear.

Psalm 112:7–8

Jesus said, "Do not be afraid. I am the First and
the Last. I am the Living One; I was dead, and
behold I am alive for ever and ever!"

Revelation 1:17–18

"I am the LORD, your God,
   who takes hold of your right hand
and says to you, Do not fear;
   I will help you,"
      declares the LORD.

Isaiah 41:13

COURAGE

God is our refuge and strength,
    an ever-present help in trouble.
Therefore we will not fear, though the earth
        give way
    and the mountains fall into the heart of the sea.

Psalm 46:1–2

The LORD will cover you with his feathers,
    and under his wings you will find refuge;
    his faithfulness will be your shield and rampart.

Psalm 91:4

God has said,
"Never will I leave you;
    never will I forsake you."
So we say with confidence,
"The Lord is my helper; I will not be afraid.
    What can man do to me?"

Hebrews 13:5–6

COURAGE

When [Elisha's servant] got up and went out early the next morning, an army with horses and chariots had surrounded the city. "Oh, my lord, what shall we do?" the servant asked.

"Don't be afraid," the prophet answered. "Those who are with us are more than those who are with them."

And Elisha prayed, "O LORD, open his eyes so he may see." Then the LORD opened the servant's eyes, and he looked and saw the hills full of horses and chariots of fire all around Elisha.

2 Kings 6:15–17

Because the hand of the LORD my God was on me, I took courage.

Ezra 7:28

COURAGE

Have no fear of sudden disaster
    or of the ruin that overtakes the wicked,
for the LORD will be your confidence
    and will keep your foot from being snared.

Proverbs 3:25–26

When I called, O LORD, you answered me;
    you made me bold and stouthearted.

Psalm 138:3

The God of all grace ... will himself restore you
and make you strong, firm and steadfast.

1 Peter 5:10

The LORD your God is the one who goes with
you to fight for you against your enemies to give
you victory.

Deuteronomy 20:4

COURAGE

I sought the LORD, and he answered me;
   he delivered me from all my fears.

Psalm 34:4

When I am afraid, O LORD,
   I will trust in you.
In God, whose word I praise,
   in God I trust; I will not be afraid.

Psalm 56:3–4

Surely God is my salvation;
   I will trust and not be afraid.
The LORD, the LORD, is my strength and my song;
   he has become my salvation.

Isaiah 12:2

COURAGE

Jesus said, "Are not two sparrows sold for a penny?
Yet not one of them will fall to the ground apart
from the will of your Father. And even the very
hairs of your head are all numbered. So don't be
afraid; you are worth more than many sparrows."

Matthew 10:29–31

**Let your hand be with me, O Lord, and keep
me from harm so that I will be free from pain.**

1 Chronicles 4:10

Reflections on
COURAGE

_____

_____

_____

_____

_____

_____

_____

_____

_____

_____

_____

_____

_____

_____

DECISIONS

Trust in the LORD with all your heart
   and lean not on your own understanding;
in all your ways acknowledge him,
   and he will make your paths straight.

Proverbs 3:5–6

The man who looks intently into the perfect law
that gives freedom, and continues to do this, not
forgetting what he has heard, but doing it—he
will be blessed in what he does.

James 1:25

A wise man listens to advice.

Proverbs 12:15

DECISIONS

If any of you lacks wisdom, he should ask God,
who gives generously to all without finding fault,
and it will be given to him.

James 1:5

The plans of the diligent lead to profit.

Proverbs 21:5

"I will counsel you and watch over you,"
		says the Lord.

Psalm 32:8

Commit to the LORD whatever you do,
		and your plans will succeed.

Proverbs 16:3

DECISIONS

In his heart a man plans his course,
    but the LORD determines his steps.

Proverbs 16:9

Those who plan what is good find love
        and faithfulness.

Proverbs 14:22

Perfume and incense bring joy to the heart,
    and the pleasantness of one's friend springs
        from his earnest counsel.

Proverbs 27:9

I am always with you, O LORD;
    you hold me by my right hand.
You guide me with your counsel,
    and afterward you will take me into glory.

Psalm 73:23–24

DECISIONS

Choose life, so that you and your children may
live and that you may love the LORD your God,
listen to his voice, and hold fast to him. For the
LORD is your life, and he will give you many years
in the land.

Deuteronomy 30:19–20

Teach me, O LORD, to follow your decrees;
   then I will keep them to the end.
Give me understanding, and I will keep your law
   and obey it with all my heart.
Direct me in the path of your commands,
   for there I find delight.

Psalm 119:33–35

Choose ... instruction instead of silver,
   knowledge rather than choice gold,
for wisdom is more precious than rubies,
   and nothing you desire can compare with her.

Proverbs 8:10–11

DECISIONS

I, wisdom, dwell together with prudence;
   I possess knowledge and discretion....
Counsel and sound judgment are mine;
   I have understanding and power.
By me kings reign
   and rulers make laws that are just;
by me princes govern,
   and all nobles who rule on earth.
I love those who love me,
   and those who seek me find me.
With me are riches and honor,
   enduring wealth and prosperity.
My fruit is better than fine gold;
   what I yield surpasses choice silver.
I walk in the way of righteousness,
   along the paths of justice,
bestowing wealth on those who love me
   and making their treasuries full.

Proverbs 8:12, 14–21

DECISIONS

Plans fail for lack of counsel,
  but with many advisers they succeed.

Proverbs 15:22

Jesus said, "I will ask the Father, and he will give
you another Counselor to be with you forever—
the Spirit of truth."

John 14:16–17

**May the LORD give you the desire of your heart
  and make all your plans succeed.**

Psalm 20:4

Reflections on
DECISIONS

_____

_____

_____

_____

_____

_____

_____

_____

_____

_____

_____

_____

_____

_____

DISCERNMENT

Praise be to the name of God for ever and ever;
    wisdom and power are his....
He gives wisdom to the wise
    and knowledge to the discerning.

Daniel 2:20–21

The Son of God has come and has given us
understanding, so that we may know him who
is true. And we are in him who is true—even in
his Son Jesus Christ. He is the true God and
eternal life.

1 John 5:20

Jesus said, "I am the way and the truth and the
life. No one comes to the Father except through
me. If you really knew me, you would know my
Father as well. From now on, you do know him
and have seen him."

John 14:6–7

DISCERNMENT

In Christ are hidden all the treasures of wisdom
and knowledge.

Colossians 2:3

No one knows the thoughts of God except the
Spirit of God. We have not received the spirit of
the world but the Spirit who is from God, that we
may understand what God has freely given us.

1 Corinthians 2:11–12

Discretion will protect you,
　　and understanding will guard you.

Proverbs 2:11

Wisdom reposes in the heart of the discerning.

Proverbs 14:33

DISCERNMENT

Preserve sound judgment and discernment,
    do not let them out of your sight;
they will be life for you,
    an ornament to grace your neck.
Then you will go on your way in safety,
    and your foot will not stumble;
when you lie down, you will not be afraid;
    when you lie down, your sleep will be sweet.

Proverbs 3:21–24

The heart of the discerning acquires knowledge;
    the ears of the wise seek it out.

Proverbs 18:15

Good understanding wins favor.

Proverbs 13:15

Understanding is a fountain of life to those who
    have it.

Proverbs 16:22

DISCERNMENT

A wise man has great power,
   and a man of knowledge increases strength.

Proverbs 24:5

**This is my prayer: that your love may abound
more and more in knowledge and depth of
insight, so that you may be able to discern
what is best and may be pure and blameless
until the day of Christ, filled with the fruit of
righteousness that comes through Jesus
Christ—to the glory and praise of God.**

Philippians 1:9–11

Reflections on
DISCERNMENT

_____

_____

_____

_____

_____

_____

_____

_____

_____

_____

_____

_____

_____

_____

_____

_____

ENCOURAGEMENT

"I know the plans I have for you," declares the
LORD, "plans to prosper you and not to harm you,
plans to give you hope and a future."

Jeremiah 29:11

God gives strength to the weary
    and increases the power of the weak.

Isaiah 40:29

You hear, O LORD, the desire of the afflicted;
    you encourage them, and you listen to their cry.

Psalm 10:17

Those who hope in the LORD
    will renew their strength.
They will soar on wings like eagles;
    they will run and not grow weary,
    they will walk and not be faint.

Isaiah 40:31

ENCOURAGEMENT

You are a shield around me, O LORD;
   you bestow glory on me and lift up my head.

Psalm 3:3

"I live in a high and holy place,
   but also with him who is contrite and lowly
      in spirit,
to revive the spirit of the lowly
   and to revive the heart of the contrite,"
      declares the LORD.

Isaiah 57:15

My purpose is that they may be encouraged in
heart and united in love, so that they may have
the full riches of complete understanding, in
order that they may know the mystery of God,
namely, Christ.

Colossians 2:2

ENCOURAGEMENT

Because God wanted to make the unchanging
nature of his purpose very clear to the heirs of
what was promised, he confirmed it with an oath.
God did this so that … we who have fled to take
hold of the hope offered to us may be greatly
encouraged. We have this hope as an anchor for
the soul, firm and secure.

Hebrews 6:17–19

The LORD upholds all those who fall
    and lifts up all who are bowed down.

Psalm 145:14

Everything that was written in the past was
written to teach us, so that through endurance
and the encouragement of the Scriptures we
might have hope.

Romans 15:4

ENCOURAGEMENT

I lift up my eyes to the hills—
  where does my help come from?
My help comes from the LORD,
  the Maker of heaven and earth.
He will not let your foot slip—
  he who watches over you will not slumber;
indeed, he who watches over Israel
  will neither slumber nor sleep.
The LORD watches over you—
  the LORD is your shade at your right hand;
the sun will not harm you by day,
  nor the moon by night.
The LORD will keep you from all harm—
  he will watch over your life;
the LORD will watch over your coming and going
  both now and forevermore.

Psalm 121

ENCOURAGEMENT

God makes my feet like the feet of a deer;
  he enables me to stand on the heights.
He trains my hands for battle;
  my arms can bend a bow of bronze.
You give me your shield of victory,
  and your right hand sustains me;
  you stoop down to make me great.
You broaden the path beneath me,
  so that my ankles do not turn.

Psalm 18:33–36

**May our Lord Jesus Christ himself and God
our Father, who loved us and by his grace gave
us eternal encouragement and good hope,
encourage your hearts and strengthen you in
every good deed and word.**

2 Thessalonians 2:16–17

Reflections on ENCOURAGEMENT

_____

_____

_____

_____

_____

_____

_____

_____

_____

_____

_____

_____

_____

_____

FAITH

Everyone born of God overcomes the world. This is the victory that has overcome the world, even our faith.

1 John 5:4

The prayer offered in faith will make the sick person well; the Lord will raise him up. If he has sinned, he will be forgiven.

James 5:15

I have fought the good fight, I have finished the race, I have kept the faith. There is in store for me the crown of righteousness, which the Lord, the righteous Judge, will award to me on that day— and not only to me, but also to all who have longed for his appearing.

2 Timothy 4:7–8

Those who have served well gain an excellent standing and great assurance in their faith in Christ Jesus.

1 Timothy 3:13

FAITH

Take up the shield of faith, with which you can extinguish all the flaming arrows of the evil one.

Ephesians 6:16

In Christ and through faith in him we may approach God with freedom and confidence.

Ephesians 3:12

You are all sons of God through faith in Christ Jesus, for all of you who were baptized into Christ have clothed yourselves with Christ.

Galatians 3:26–27

God redeemed us . . . so that by faith we might receive the promise of the Spirit.

Galatians 3:14

A faithful man will be richly blessed.

Proverbs 28:20

FAITH

The life I live in the body, I live by faith in the
Son of God, who loved me and gave himself
for me.

Galatians 2:20

Since we have been justified through faith, we
have peace with God through our Lord Jesus
Christ, through whom we have gained access by
faith into this grace in which we now stand. And
we rejoice in the hope of the glory of God.

Romans 5:1–2

Jesus said, "I tell you the truth, anyone who has
faith in me will do what I have been doing. He
will do even greater things than these, because I
am going to the Father."

John 14:12

FAITH

Jesus said, "If you have faith as small as a mustard seed, you can say to this mountain, 'Move from here to there' and it will move. Nothing will be impossible for you."

Matthew 17:20

Those who have faith are blessed.

Galatians 3:9

Righteousness from God comes through faith in Jesus Christ to all who believe.

Romans 3:22

The LORD is faithful to all his promises
and loving toward all he has made.

Psalm 145:13

FAITH

I do not have time to tell about Gideon, Barak, Samson, Jephthah, David, Samuel and the prophets, who through faith conquered kingdoms, administered justice, and gained what was promised; who shut the mouths of lions, quenched the fury of the flames, and escaped the edge of the sword; whose weakness was turned to strength; and who became powerful in battle and routed foreign armies. ... The world was not worthy of them. ... These were all commended for their faith.

Hebrews 11:32–33, 34, 38–39

I pray that out of God's glorious riches he may strengthen you with power through his Spirit in your inner being, so that Christ may dwell in your hearts through faith.

Ephesians 3:16–17

Reflections on
FAITH

_____

_____

_____

_____

_____

_____

_____

_____

_____

_____

_____

_____

_____

_____

_____

_____

_____

FATHERHOOD

From everlasting to everlasting
   the LORD's love is with those who fear him,
   and his righteousness with their children's
      children—
with those who keep his covenant
   and remember to obey his precepts.

Psalm 103:17–18

Parents are the pride of their children.

Proverbs 17:6

Fathers tell their children
   about your faithfulness, O LORD.

Isaiah 38:19

FATHERHOOD

Blessed is the man who fears the LORD,
  who finds great delight in his commands.
His children will be mighty in the land;
  the generation of the upright will be blessed.

Psalm 112:1–2

O my people, hear my teaching;
  listen to the words of my mouth.
I will open my mouth in parables,
  I will utter hidden things, things from of old—
what we have heard and known,
  what our fathers have told us.
We will not hide them from their children;
  we will tell the next generation
the praiseworthy deeds of the LORD,
  his power, and the wonders he has done.

Psalm 78:1–4

FATHERHOOD

Repent and be baptized, every one of you, in the
name of Jesus Christ for the forgiveness of your
sins. And you will receive the gift of the Holy
Spirit. The promise is for you and your children.

Acts 2:38–39

We have all had human fathers who disciplined us
and we respected them for it. How much more
should we submit to the Father of our spirits and
live! Our fathers disciplined us for a little while as
they thought best; but God disciplines us for our
good, that we may share in his holiness. No
discipline seems pleasant at the time, but painful.
Later on, however, it produces a harvest of
righteousness and peace for those who have been
trained by it.

Hebrews 12:9–11

FATHERHOOD

Jesus said, "Which of you fathers, if your son asks
for a fish, will give him a snake instead? Or if he
asks for an egg, will give him a scorpion? If you
then ... know how to give good gifts to your
children, how much more will your Father in
heaven give the Holy Spirit to those who ask him!"

Luke 11:11–13

Keep God's decrees and commands ... so that it
may go well with you and your children after you
and that you may live long in the land.

Deuteronomy 4:40

The righteous man leads a blameless life;
blessed are his children after him.

Proverbs 20:7

FATHERHOOD

Teach [God's words] to your children, talking
about them when you sit at home and when you
walk along the road, when you lie down and
when you get up. Write them on the doorframes
of your houses and on your gates, so that your
days and the days of your children may be many
in the land that the LORD swore to give your
forefathers, as many as the days that the heavens
are above the earth.

Deuteronomy 11:19–21

He who fears the LORD has a secure fortress,
　　and for his children it will be a refuge.

Proverbs 14:26

"I will contend with those who contend with you,
　　and your children I will save,"
　　　　declares the LORD.

Isaiah 49:25

FATHERHOOD

"I will give them singleness of heart and action, so that they will always fear me for their own good and the good of their children after them. I will make an everlasting covenant with them: I will never stop doing good to them, and I will inspire them to fear me, so that they will never turn away from me," says the LORD.

Jeremiah 32:39–40

May the LORD make you increase,
    both you and your children.
May you be blessed by the LORD,
    the Maker of heaven and earth.

Psalm 115:14–15

Reflections on
FATHERHOOD

_____

_____

_____

_____

_____

_____

_____

_____

_____

_____

_____

_____

_____

_____

_____

_____

FORGIVENESS

If we confess our sins, God is faithful and just and will forgive us our sins and purify us from all unrighteousness.

1 John 1:9

If you forgive men when they sin against you, your heavenly Father will also forgive you.

Matthew 6:14

Blessed are the merciful,
    for they will be shown mercy.

Matthew 5:7

Blessed is he
    whose transgressions are forgiven,
    whose sins are covered.

Psalm 32:1

FORGIVENESS

The LORD is compassionate and gracious,
    slow to anger, abounding in love.
He will not always accuse,
    nor will he harbor his anger forever;
he does not treat us as our sins deserve
    or repay us according to our iniquities.
For as high as the heavens are above the earth,
    so great is his love for those who fear him;
as far as the east is from the west,
    so far has he removed our transgressions
       from us.
As a father has compassion on his children,
    so the LORD has compassion on those who
       fear him.

Psalm 103:8–13

FORGIVENESS

"Come now, let us reason together,"
   says the LORD.
"Though your sins are like scarlet,
   they shall be as white as snow;
though they are red as crimson,
   they shall be like wool."

Isaiah 1:18

Have mercy on me, O God,
   according to your unfailing love;
according to your great compassion
   blot out my transgressions.
Wash away all my iniquity
   and cleanse me from my sin.

Psalm 51:1–2

Cleanse me with hyssop, O LORD, and I will
      be clean;
   wash me, and I will be whiter than snow.

Psalm 51:7

FORGIVENESS

Confess your sins to each other and pray for each other so that you may be healed.

James 5:16

In Christ we have redemption through his blood, the forgiveness of sins, in accordance with the riches of God's grace that he lavished on us with all wisdom and understanding.

Ephesians 1:7–8

You were washed, you were sanctified, you were justified in the name of the Lord Jesus Christ and by the Spirit of our God.

1 Corinthians 6:11

All the prophets testify about Jesus that everyone who believes in him receives forgiveness of sins through his name.

Acts 10:43

FORGIVENESS

Who is a God like you,
    who pardons sin and forgives the transgression
    of the remnant of his inheritance?
You do not stay angry forever
    but delight to show mercy.
You will again have compassion on us;
    you will tread our sins underfoot
    and hurl all our iniquities into the depths of
        the sea.

Micah 7:18–19

God forgave us all our sins, having canceled the
written code, with its regulations, that was against
us and that stood opposed to us; he took it away,
nailing it to the cross.

Colossians 2:13–14

FORGIVENESS

God has rescued us from the dominion of
darkness and brought us into the kingdom of the
Son he loves, in whom we have redemption, the
forgiveness of sins.

Colossians 1:13–14

If you, O LORD, kept a record of sins,
   O Lord, who could stand?
But with you there is forgiveness.

Psalm 130:3–4

We have now been justified by Christ's blood.

Romans 5:9

Christ is the atoning sacrifice for our sins,
and not only for ours but also for the sins of
the whole world.

1 John 2:2

FORGIVENESS

Through Christ we have now received
reconciliation.

Romans 5:11

Whoever believes in Jesus is not condemned.

John 3:18

Repent... and turn to God, so that your sins may
be wiped out, that times of refreshing may come
from the Lord.

Acts 3:19

Create in me a pure heart, O God,
   and renew a steadfast spirit within me.
Do not cast me from your presence
   or take your Holy Spirit from me.
Restore to me the joy of your salvation
   and grant me a willing spirit, to sustain me.

Psalm 51:10–12

Reflections on
FORGIVENESS

_____

_____

_____

_____

_____

_____

_____

_____

_____

_____

_____

_____

_____

_____

_____

_____

_____

_____

FRIENDSHIP

A friend loves at all times,
and a brother is born for adversity.

Proverbs 17:17

A man of many companions may come to ruin,
but there is a friend who sticks closer than
a brother.

Proverbs 18:24

He who loves a pure heart and whose speech
is gracious
will have the king for his friend.

Proverbs 22:11

Perfume and incense bring joy to the heart,
and the pleasantness of one's friend springs
from his earnest counsel.

Proverbs 27:9

FRIENDSHIP

Two are better than one,
 because they have a good return for their work:
If one falls down,
 his friend can help him up.
But pity the man who falls
 and has no one to help him up!
Also, if two lie down together, they will
 keep warm.
 But how can one keep warm alone?
Though one may be overpowered,
 two can defend themselves.
A cord of three strands is not quickly broken.

Ecclesiastes 4:9–12

Wounds from a friend can be trusted.

Proverbs 27:6

FRIENDSHIP

Jesus said, "Greater love has no one than this, that he lay down his life for his friends. You are my friends if you do what I command. I no longer call you servants, because a servant does not know his master's business. Instead, I have called you friends, for everything that I learned from my Father I have made known to you."

John 15:13–15

Dear friend, I pray that you may enjoy good health and that all may go well with you, even as your soul is getting along well.

3 John 1:2

Reflections on
FRIENDSHIP

_____

_____

_____

_____

_____

_____

_____

_____

_____

_____

_____

_____

_____

_____

_____

_____

_____

_____

_____

FUTURE

O LORD, you have made known to me the path
     of life;
  you will fill me with joy in your presence,
          with eternal pleasures at your right hand.

Psalm 16:11

It is God who makes . . . you stand firm in Christ.
He anointed us, set his seal of ownership on us,
and put his Spirit in our hearts as a deposit,
guaranteeing what is to come.

2 Corinthians 1:21–22

"Forget the former things;
   do not dwell on the past.
See, I am doing a new thing!
   Now it springs up; do you not perceive it?
I am making a way in the desert
   and streams in the wasteland,"
      declares the Lord.

Isaiah 43:18–19

FUTURE

I saw a new heaven and a new earth, for the first
heaven and the first earth had passed away, and
there was no longer any sea. I saw the Holy City,
the new Jerusalem, coming down out of heaven
from God, prepared as a bride beautifully dressed
for her husband. And I heard a loud voice from
the throne saying, "Now the dwelling of God is
with men, and he will live with them. They will
be his people, and God himself will be with them
and be their God. He will wipe every tear from
their eyes. There will be no more death or
mourning or crying or pain, for the old order of
things has passed away."

Revelation 21:1–4

If anyone is in Christ, he is a new creation; the old
has gone, the new has come!

2 Corinthians 5:17

FUTURE

All the days ordained for me
   were written in your book, O LORD,
   before one of them came to be.

Psalm 139:16

It is written: "No eye has seen, no ear has heard,
no mind has conceived what God has prepared for
those who love him"—but God has revealed it to
us by his Spirit.

1 Corinthians 2:9

Now we are children of God, and what we will be
has not yet been made known. But we know that
when Christ appears, we shall be like him, for we
shall see him as he is.

1 John 3:2

The blameless will receive a good inheritance.

Proverbs 28:10

FUTURE

"As the new heavens and the new earth that I
make will endure before me," declares the LORD,
"so will your name and descendants endure."

Isaiah 66:22

The God of heaven will set up a kingdom that
will never be destroyed.

Daniel 2:44

"My Spirit, who is on you, and my words that I
have put in your mouth will not depart from your
mouth, or from the mouths of your children, or
from the mouths of their descendants from this
time on and forever," says the LORD.

Isaiah 59:21

Jesus is coming with the clouds,
    and every eye will see him.

Revelation 1:7

FUTURE

One generation will commend your works to
    another;
  they will tell of your mighty acts, O LORD.
They will speak of the glorious splendor of
    your majesty,
  and I will meditate on your wonderful works.
They will tell of the power of your awesome works,
  and I will proclaim your great deeds.
They will celebrate your abundant goodness
  and joyfully sing of your righteousness.

Psalm 145:4–7

FUTURE

All things are yours, whether . . . the world or life
or death or the present or the future—all are
yours, and you are of Christ, and Christ is of God.

1 Corinthians 3:21–23

Our citizenship is in heaven. And we eagerly await
a Savior from there, the Lord Jesus Christ, who,
by the power that enables him to bring everything
under his control, will transform our lowly bodies
so that they will be like his glorious body.

Philippians 3:20–21

Even when I am old and gray,
   do not forsake me, O God,
till I declare your power to the next generation,
   your might to all who are to come.
Your righteousness reaches to the skies, O God,
   you who have done great things.
Who, O God, is like you?

Psalm 71:18–19

Reflections on the FUTURE

_____

_____

_____

_____

_____

_____

_____

_____

_____

_____

_____

_____

_____

_____

_____

_____

_____

_____

GOD'S LOVE

God so loved the world that he gave his one and
only Son, that whoever believes in him shall not
perish but have eternal life.

John 3:16

Dear friends, let us love one another, for love
comes from God. Everyone who loves has been
born of God and knows God.

1 John 4:7

The LORD tends his flock like a shepherd:
  He gathers the lambs in his arms
and carries them close to his heart;
  he gently leads those that have young.

Isaiah 40:11

This is how God showed his love among us: He
sent his one and only Son into the world that we
might live through him.

1 John 4:9

GOD'S LOVE

The eyes of the LORD are on those who fear him,
   on those whose hope is in his unfailing love.

Psalm 33:18

We love because God first loved us.

1 John 4:19

Your love, O LORD, reaches to the heavens,
   your faithfulness to the skies.

Psalm 36:5

By day the LORD directs his love,
   at night his song is with me—
   a prayer to the God of my life.

Psalm 42:8

This is love: not that we loved God, but that he
loved us and sent his Son as an atoning sacrifice
for our sins.

1 John 4:10

GOD'S LOVE

I will praise you, O Lord, among the nations;
  I will sing of you among the peoples.
For great is your love, reaching to the heavens;
  your faithfulness reaches to the skies.

Psalm 57:9–10

One thing God has spoken,
  two things have I heard:
that you, O God, are strong,
  and that you, O Lord, are loving.
Surely you will reward each person
  according to what he has done.

Psalm 62:11–12

If we love one another, God lives in us and his
love is made complete in us.

1 John 4:12

GOD'S LOVE

I have seen you in the sanctuary, O LORD,
  and beheld your power and your glory.
Because your love is better than life,
  my lips will glorify you.
I will praise you as long as I live,
  and in your name I will lift up my hands.

Psalm 63:2–4

Give thanks to the LORD, for he is good;
  his love endures forever.

1 Chronicles 16:34

"Though the mountains be shaken
  and the hills be removed,
yet my unfailing love for you will not be shaken
  nor my covenant of peace be removed,"
  says the LORD, who has compassion on you.

Isaiah 54:10

GOD'S LOVE

The LORD will take great delight in you,
　　he will quiet you with his love,
　　　he will rejoice over you with singing.

Zephaniah 3:17

We know and rely on the love God has for us.

1 John 4:16

I will sing of the LORD's great love forever;
　　with my mouth I will make your faithfulness
　　　known through all generations.
I will declare that your love stands firm forever,
　　that you established your faithfulness in
　　　　heaven itself.

Psalm 89:1–2

The LORD is good to all;
　　he has compassion on all he has made.

Psalm 145:9

GOD'S LOVE

Whoever lives in love lives in God, and God in him. In this way, love is made complete among us so that we will have confidence on the day of judgment, because in this world we are like him.

1 John 4:16–17

Jesus said, "I am the good shepherd. The good shepherd lays down his life for the sheep."

John 10:11

Neither death nor life, neither angels nor demons, neither the present nor the future, nor any powers, neither height nor depth, nor anything else in all creation, will be able to separate us from the love of God that is in Christ Jesus our Lord.

Romans 8:38–39

GOD'S LOVE

The LORD disciplines those he loves,
    as a father the son he delights in.

Proverbs 3:12

God will show compassion,
    so great is his unfailing love.

Lamentations 3:32

Righteousness and justice are the foundation of
       your throne;
    love and faithfulness go before you, O LORD.

Psalm 89:14

**O LORD, God of Israel, there is no God like
you in heaven above or on earth below—you
who keep your covenant of love with your
servants who continue wholeheartedly in
your way.**

1 Kings 8:23

Reflections on
GOD'S LOVE

_____

_____

_____

_____

_____

_____

_____

_____

_____

_____

_____

_____

_____

_____

_____

_____

_____

GRACE

Jesus said, "My grace is sufficient for you, for my power is made perfect in weakness." Therefore I will boast all the more gladly about my weaknesses, so that Christ's power may rest on me.

2 Corinthians 12:9

The grace of God that brings salvation has appeared to all men. It teaches us to say "No" to ungodliness and worldly passions, and to live self-controlled, upright and godly lives in this present age, while we wait for the blessed hope—the glorious appearing of our great God and Savior, Jesus Christ, who gave himself for us to redeem us from all wickedness and to purify for himself a people that are his very own, eager to do what is good.

Titus 2:11–14

GRACE

When the kindness and love of God our Savior
appeared, he saved us, not because of righteous
things we had done, but because of his mercy. He
saved us through the washing of rebirth and
renewal by the Holy Spirit, whom he poured out
on us generously through Jesus Christ our Savior,
so that, having been justified by his grace, we
might become heirs having the hope of eternal life.

Titus 3:4–7

Where sin increased, grace increased all the more,
so that, just as sin reigned in death, so also grace
might reign through righteousness to bring eternal
life through Jesus Christ our Lord.

Romans 5:20–21

God is able to make all grace abound to you, so
that in all things at all times, having all that you
need, you will abound in every good work.

2 Corinthians 9:8

GRACE

Because of his great love for us, God, who is rich
in mercy, made us alive with Christ even when we
were dead in transgressions—it is by grace you
have been saved. And God raised us up with
Christ and seated us with him in the heavenly
realms in Christ Jesus, in order that in the coming
ages he might show the incomparable riches of
his grace, expressed in his kindness to us in
Christ Jesus.

Ephesians 2:4–7

If, by the trespass of the one man, death reigned
through that one man, how much more will those
who receive God's abundant provision of grace
and of the gift of righteousness reign in life
through the one man, Jesus Christ.

Romans 5:17

GRACE

The LORD is gracious and righteous;
   our God is full of compassion.

Psalm 116:5

You know the grace of our Lord Jesus Christ, that
though he was rich, yet for your sakes he became
poor, so that you through his poverty might
become rich.

2 Corinthians 8:9

The LORD longs to be gracious to you;
   he rises to show you compassion.
For the LORD is a God of justice.
   Blessed are all who wait for him!

Isaiah 30:18

From the fullness of God's grace we have all
received one blessing after another.

John 1:16

GRACE

All are justified freely by God's grace through the redemption that came by Christ Jesus.

Romans 3:24

How gracious God will be when you cry for help! As soon as he hears, he will answer you.

Isaiah 30:19

God chose us in him before the creation of the world to be holy and blameless in his sight. In love he predestined us to be adopted as his sons through Jesus Christ, in accordance with his pleasure and will—to the praise of his glorious grace, which he has freely given us in the One he loves. In him we have redemption through his blood, the forgiveness of sins, in accordance with the riches of God's grace that he lavished on us with all wisdom and understanding.

Ephesians 1:4–8

GRACE

God who did not spare his own Son, but gave him up for us all—how will he not also, along with him, graciously give us all things?

Romans 8:32

We have different gifts, according to the grace given us.

Romans 12:6

The grace of our Lord was poured out on me abundantly, along with the faith and love that are in Christ Jesus. Here is a trustworthy saying that deserves full acceptance: Christ Jesus came into the world to save sinners—of whom I am the worst. But for that very reason I was shown mercy so that in me, the worst of sinners, Christ Jesus might display his unlimited patience as an example for those who would believe on him and receive eternal life.

1 Timothy 1:14–16

GRACE

God, ... has saved us and called us to a holy life—
not because of anything we have done but because
of his own purpose and grace. This grace was
given us in Christ Jesus before the beginning of
time, but it has now been revealed through the
appearing of our Savior, Christ Jesus, who has
destroyed death and has brought life and
immortality to light through the gospel.

2 Timothy 1:8–10

To each one of us grace has been given as Christ
apportioned it.

Ephesians 4:7

Grace, mercy and peace from God the Father and
from Jesus Christ, the Father's Son, will be with us
in truth and love.

2 John 1:3

GRACE

Let us ... approach the throne of grace with
confidence, so that we may receive mercy and find
grace to help us in our time of need.

Hebrews 4:16

We see Jesus, who was made a little lower than the
angels, now crowned with glory and honor
because he suffered death, so that by the grace of
God he might taste death for everyone.

Hebrews 2:9

**Grace and peace be yours in abundance
through the knowledge of God and of Jesus
our Lord.**

2 Peter 1:2

Reflections on
GRACE

_____

_____

_____

_____

_____

_____

_____

_____

_____

_____

_____

_____

_____

_____

_____

GUIDANCE

The LORD is my shepherd, I shall not be in want.
   He makes me lie down in green pastures,
he leads me beside quiet waters,
   he restores my soul.
He guides me in paths of righteousness
   for his name's sake.

Psalm 23:1–3

God is our God for ever and ever;
   he will be our guide even to the end.

Psalm 48:14

Your word, O LORD, is a lamp to my feet
   and a light for my path.

Psalm 119:105

O LORD, you have made known to me the path
     of life.

Psalm 16:11

GUIDANCE

The law of the LORD is perfect,
reviving the soul.
The statutes of the LORD are trustworthy,
making wise the simple.
The precepts of the LORD are right,
giving joy to the heart.
The commands of the LORD are radiant,
giving light to the eyes.
The fear of the LORD is pure,
enduring forever.
The ordinances of the LORD are sure
and altogether righteous.
They are more precious than gold,
than much pure gold;
they are sweeter than honey,
than honey from the comb.
By them is your servant warned;
in keeping them there is great reward.

Psalm 19:7–11

GUIDANCE

Jesus said, "I am the light of the world. Whoever follows me will never walk in darkness, but will have the light of life."

John 8:12

God is light; in him there is no darkness at all. . . . If we walk in the light, as he is in the light, we have fellowship with one another, and the blood of Jesus, his Son, purifies us from all sin.

1 John 1:5, 7

Jesus said, "If you hold to my teaching, you are really my disciples. Then you will know the truth, and the truth will set you free."

John 8:31–32

The path of the righteous is like the first gleam
      of dawn,
    shining ever brighter till the full light of day.

Proverbs 4:18

GUIDANCE

This is what the LORD says—
    your Redeemer, the Holy One of Israel:
"I am the LORD your God,
    who teaches you what is best for you,
    who directs you in the way you should go."

Isaiah 48:17

I guide you in the way of wisdom
    and lead you along straight paths.
When you walk, your steps will not be hampered;
    when you run, you will not stumble.

Proverbs 4:11–12

"I will instruct you and teach you in the way
    you should go," says the Lord.

Psalm 32:8

GUIDANCE

I will praise the LORD, who counsels me;
  even at night my heart instructs me.

Psalm 16:7

When he, the Spirit of truth, comes, he will guide
you into all truth. He will not speak on his own;
he will speak only what he hears, and he will tell
you what is yet to come.

John 16:13

Hold on to instruction, do not let it go;
  guard it well, for it is your life.

Proverbs 4:13

He who listens to a life-giving rebuke
  will be at home among the wise.

Proverbs 15:31

GUIDANCE

Whether you turn to the right or to the left, your ears will hear a voice behind you, saying, "This is the way; walk in it."

Isaiah 30:21

He who walks with the wise grows wise.

Proverbs 13:20

Teach me to do your will, O LORD,
**   for you are my God;**
may your good Spirit
**   lead me on level ground.**

Psalm 143:10

Reflections on
GUIDANCE

HEALING

Praise the LORD, O my soul;
  all my inmost being, praise his holy name.
Praise the LORD, O my soul,
  and forget not all his benefits—
who forgives all your sins
  and heals all your diseases,
who redeems your life from the pit
  and crowns you with love and compassion,
who satisfies your desires with good things
  so that your youth is renewed like the eagle's.

Psalm 103:1–5

"I will bind up the injured and strengthen the
weak," declares the Sovereign LORD.

Ezekiel 34:16

HEALING

"For you who revere my name, the sun of righteousness will rise with healing in its wings," says the LORD Almighty.

Malachi 4:2

God heals the brokenhearted
and binds up their wounds.

Psalm 147:3

"I will heal my people and will let them enjoy abundant peace and security," declares the LORD.

Jeremiah 33:6

"I will restore you to health
and heal your wounds,"
declares the LORD.

Jeremiah 30:17

HEALING

The prayer offered in faith will make the sick
person well; the Lord will raise him up.

James 5:15

O LORD my God, I called to you for help
   and you healed me.

Psalm 30:2

"Your light will break forth like the dawn,
   and your healing will quickly appear,"
      declares the LORD.

Isaiah 58:8

"If my people, who are called by my name, will
humble themselves and pray and seek my face and
turn from their wicked ways, then will I hear from
heaven and will forgive their sin and will heal their
land," says the Lord.

2 Chronicles 7:14

HEALING

Surely the Messiah took up our infirmities
   and carried our sorrows....
But he was pierced for our transgressions,
   he was crushed for our iniquities;
the punishment that brought us peace was
     upon him,
   and by his wounds we are healed.

Isaiah 53:4–5

Confess your sins to each other and pray for each
other so that you may be healed. The prayer of a
righteous man is powerful and effective.

James 5:16

Christ himself bore our sins in his body on
the tree, so that we might die to sins and live
for righteousness; by his wounds you have
been healed.

1 Peter 2:24

HEALING

The God of all grace, who called you to his eternal
glory in Christ, after you have suffered a little
while, will himself restore you and make you
strong, firm and steadfast.

1 Peter 5:10

You will restore my life again, O Lord;
from the depths of the earth
   you will again bring me up.
You will increase my honor
   and comfort me once again.

Psalm 71:20–21

**I pray that you may enjoy good health and that
all may go well with you, even as your soul is
getting along well.**

3 John 1:2

Reflections on
HEALING

_____

_____

_____

_____

_____

_____

_____

_____

_____

_____

_____

_____

_____

_____

_____

HELP

I lift up my eyes to the hills—
   where does my help come from?
My help comes from the LORD,
   the Maker of heaven and earth.

Psalm 121:1–2

God is able to do immeasurably more than all we
ask or imagine.

Ephesians 3:20

On my bed I remember you, O LORD;
   I think of you through the watches of the night.
Because you are my help,
   I sing in the shadow of your wings.
My soul clings to you;
   your right hand upholds me.

Psalm 63:6–8

HELP

Nothing is impossible with God.

Luke 1:37

Jesus said, "I am the vine; you are the branches. If a man remains in me and I in him, he will bear much fruit.... If you remain in me and my words remain in you, ask whatever you wish, and it will be given you."

John 15:5, 7

If the LORD delights in a man's way,
    he makes his steps firm;
though he stumble, he will not fall,
    for the LORD upholds him with his hand.

Psalm 37:23–24

You, O God, do see trouble and grief;
    you consider it to take it in hand.

Psalm 10:14

HELP

A righteous man may have many troubles,
    but the LORD delivers him from them all.

Psalm 34:19

I waited patiently for the LORD;
    he turned to me and heard my cry.
He lifted me out of the slimy pit,
    out of the mud and mire;
he set my feet on a rock
    and gave me a firm place to stand.

Psalm 40:1–2

God is our refuge and strength,
    an ever-present help in trouble.
Therefore we will not fear, though the earth
      give way
    and the mountains fall into the heart of the sea,
though its waters roar and foam
    and the mountains quake with their surging.

Psalm 46:1–3

HELP

"Call upon me in the day of trouble;
   I will deliver you, and you will honor me,"
      declares the LORD.

Psalm 50:15

Surely God is my help;
   the Lord is the one who sustains me.

Psalm 54:4

Praise be to the Lord, to God our Savior,
   who daily bears our burdens.

Psalm 68:19

The LORD your God is with you,
   he is mighty to save.

Zephaniah 3:17

HELP

I am the LORD, your God,
  who takes hold of your right hand
and says to you, Do not fear;
  I will help you.

Isaiah 41:13

Blessed is he whose help is the God of Jacob,
  whose hope is in the LORD his God,
the Maker of heaven and earth,
  the sea, and everything in them—
  the LORD, who remains faithful forever.
He upholds the cause of the oppressed
  and gives food to the hungry.
The LORD sets prisoners free,
  the LORD gives sight to the blind,
the LORD lifts up those who are bowed down,
  the LORD loves the righteous.

Psalm 146:5–8

HELP

With your help, O LORD, I can advance
    against a troop;
  with my God I can scale a wall.

2 Samuel 22:30

God will deliver the needy who cry out.

Psalm 72:12

The LORD helps [the righteous] and delivers them.

Psalm 37:40

The LORD has not despised or disdained
    the suffering of the afflicted one;
he has not hidden his face from him
    but has listened to his cry for help.

Psalm 22:24

Because he himself suffered when he was tempted,
Jesus is able to help those who are being tempted.

Hebrews 2:18

HELP

"I will refresh the weary and satisfy the faint," says
the LORD.

Jeremiah 31:25

You, O LORD, have helped me and comforted me.

Psalm 86:17

In the day of my trouble I will call to you,
       O LORD,
   for you will answer me.

Psalm 86:7

May the LORD send you help
       from the sanctuary
and grant you support from Zion.

Psalm 20:2

Reflections on
HELP

_____

_____

_____

_____

_____

_____

_____

_____

_____

_____

_____

_____

_____

_____

_____

_____

_____

HOPE

I am the LORD;
    those who hope in me will not be disappointed.

Isaiah 49:23

Let us hold unswervingly to the hope we profess,
for God who promised is faithful.

Hebrews 10:23

"I know the plans I have for you," declares the
LORD, "plans to prosper you and not to harm you,
plans to give you hope and a future."

Jeremiah 29:11

Weeping may remain for a night,
    but rejoicing comes in the morning.

Psalm 30:5

HOPE

Those who sow in tears
    will reap with songs of joy.
He who goes out weeping,
    carrying seed to sow,
will return with songs of joy,
    carrying sheaves with him.

Psalm 126:5–6

You have been my hope, O Sovereign LORD,
    my confidence since my youth.
From birth I have relied on you;
    you brought me forth from my mother's womb.
    I will ever praise you.

Psalm 71:5–6

I watch in hope for the LORD,
    I wait for God my Savior;
    my God will hear me.

Micah 7:7

HOPE

This I call to mind
    and therefore I have hope:
Because of the LORD's great love we are
        not consumed,
    for his compassions never fail.
They are new every morning;
    great is your faithfulness, O LORD.

Lamentations 3:21–23

We rejoice in the hope of the glory of God. Not
only so, but we also rejoice in our sufferings,
because we know that suffering produces
perseverance; perseverance, character; and
character, hope. And hope does not disappoint us,
because God has poured out his love into our
hearts by the Holy Spirit, whom he has given us.

Romans 5:2–5

HOPE

The LORD is good to those whose hope is in him,
　to the one who seeks him;
it is good to wait quietly
　for the salvation of the LORD.

Lamentations 3:25–26

Find rest, O my soul, in God alone;
　my hope comes from him.

Psalm 62:5

Those who hope in the LORD will inherit
　　the land.

Psalm 37:9

You know with all your heart and soul that not
one of all the good promises the LORD your God
gave you has failed. Every promise has been
fulfilled; not one has failed.

Joshua 23:14

HOPE

No one whose hope is in you, Lord,
　　will ever be put to shame.

Psalm 25:3

The eyes of the LORD are on those who fear him,
　　on those whose hope is in his unfailing love,

Psalm 33:18

God has delivered us from such a deadly peril, and
he will deliver us. On him we have set our hope
that he will continue to deliver us.

2 Corinthians 1:10

There is surely a future hope for you,
　　and your hope will not be cut off.

Proverbs 23:18

HOPE

Those who hope in the LORD
will renew their strength.
They will soar on wings like eagles;
they will run and not grow weary,
they will walk and not be faint.

Isaiah 40:31

The LORD delights in those who fear him,
who put their hope in his unfailing love.

Psalm 147:11

Command those who are rich in this present
world not to be arrogant nor to put their hope in
wealth, which is so uncertain, but to put their
hope in God, who richly provides us with
everything for our enjoyment.

1 Timothy 6:17

HOPE

When the kindness and love of God our Savior
appeared, he saved us, not because of righteous
things we had done, but because of his mercy.
He saved us through the washing of rebirth and
renewal by the Holy Spirit, whom he poured out
on us generously through Jesus Christ our Savior,
so that, having been justified by his grace, we
might become heirs having the hope of eternal life.

Titus 3:4–7

**May the God of hope fill you with all joy and
peace as you trust in him, so that you may
overflow with hope by the power of the
Holy Spirit.**

Romans 15:13

Reflections on
HOPE

_____
_____
_____
_____
_____
_____
_____
_____
_____
_____
_____
_____
_____
_____
_____
_____
_____

IDENTITY

When God created man, he made him in the
likeness of God.

Genesis 5:1

We are God's workmanship, created in Christ
Jesus to do good works, which God prepared in
advance for us to do.

Ephesians 2:10

The LORD God formed the man from the dust of
the ground and breathed into his nostrils the
breath of life, and the man became a living being.

Genesis 2:7

How great is the love the Father has lavished on
us, that we should be called children of God! And
that is what we are!

1 John 3:1

IDENTITY

You created my inmost being, O LORD;
     you knit me together in my mother's womb.
I praise you because I am fearfully and
          wonderfully made;
     your works are wonderful,
     I know that full well.
My frame was not hidden from you
     when I was made in the secret place.
When I was woven together in the depths of
          the earth,
     your eyes saw my unformed body.
All the days ordained for me
     were written in your book
     before one of them came to be.

Psalm 139:13–16

IDENTITY

What is man that you are mindful of him,
    the son of man that you care for him?
You made him a little lower than
      the heavenly beings
    and crowned him with glory and honor.
You made him ruler over the works of your hands;
    you put everything under his feet:
all flocks and herds,
    and the beasts of the field,
the birds of the air,
    and the fish of the sea,
    all that swim the paths of the seas.
O LORD, our Lord,
    how majestic is your name in all the earth!

Psalm 8:4–9

IDENTITY

Praise be to the God and Father of our Lord Jesus
Christ, who has blessed us in the heavenly realms
with every spiritual blessing in Christ. For he
chose us in him before the creation of the world
to be holy and blameless in his sight. In love he
predestined us to be adopted as his sons through
Jesus Christ, in accordance with his pleasure and
will—to the praise of his glorious grace, which he
has freely given us in the One he loves.

Ephesians 1:3–6

Those who are led by the Spirit of God are sons
of God. For you did not receive a spirit that
makes you a slave again to fear, but you received
the Spirit of sonship. And by him we cry, *"Abba,
Father."* The Spirit himself testifies with our
spirit that we are God's children. Now if we are
children, then we are heirs—heirs of God and
co-heirs with Christ.

Romans 8:14–17

IDENTITY

You are all sons of God through faith in Christ Jesus, for all of you who were baptized into Christ have clothed yourselves with Christ. There is neither Jew nor Greek, slave nor free, male nor female, for you are all one in Christ Jesus. If you belong to Christ, then you are Abraham's seed, and heirs according to the promise.

Galatians 3:26–29

You are no longer foreigners and aliens, but fellow citizens with God's people and members of God's household, built on the foundation of the apostles and prophets, with Christ Jesus himself as the chief cornerstone. In him the whole building is joined together and rises to become a holy temple in the Lord. And in him you too are being built together to become a dwelling in which God lives by his Spirit.

Ephesians 2:19–22

IDENTITY

You yourselves are God's temple and … God's
Spirit lives in you.

1 Corinthians 3:16

If anyone is in Christ, he is a new creation; the old
has gone, the new has come!

2 Corinthians 5:17

Jesus said, "I no longer call you servants, because a
servant does not know his master's business.
Instead, I have called you friends, for everything
that I learned from my Father I have made known
to you."

John 15:15

You are a chosen people, a royal priesthood, a holy
nation, a people belonging to God, that you may
declare the praises of him who called you out of
darkness into his wonderful light.

1 Peter 2:9

IDENTITY

You are all sons of the light and sons of the day.

1 Thessalonians 5:5

You are the body of Christ, and each one of you is a part of it.

1 Corinthians 12:27

You show that you are a letter from Christ, . . . written not with ink but with the Spirit of the living God, not on tablets of stone but on tablets of human hearts.

2 Corinthians 3:3

I pray . . . that the eyes of your heart may be enlightened in order that you may know the hope to which God has called you, the riches of his glorious inheritance in the saints, and his incomparably great power for us who believe.

Ephesians 1:18–19

Reflections on
IDENTITY

_____

_____

_____

_____

_____

_____

_____

_____

_____

_____

_____

_____

_____

_____

_____

_____

_____

_____

INTEGRITY

The righteous man leads a blameless life;
   blessed are his children after him.

Proverbs 20:7

I the LORD search the heart
   and examine the mind,
to reward a man according to his conduct,
   according to what his deeds deserve.

Jeremiah 17:10

The LORD blesses the home of the righteous.

Proverbs 3:33

The man of integrity walks securely.

Proverbs 10:9

INTEGRITY

LORD, who may dwell in your sanctuary?
  Who may live on your holy hill?
He whose walk is blameless
  and who does what is righteous,
who speaks the truth from his heart
  and has no slander on his tongue,
who does his neighbor no wrong
  and casts no slur on his fellowman,
who despises a vile man
  but honors those who fear the LORD,
who keeps his oath
  even when it hurts,
who lends his money without usury
  and does not accept a bribe
    against the innocent.
He who does these things
  will never be shaken.

Psalm 15

INTEGRITY

The LORD is righteous,
   he loves justice;
     upright men will see his face.

Psalm 11:7

Blessed are those who have learned to acclaim you,
   who walk in the light of your presence,
      O LORD.

Psalm 89:15

He who does what is right is righteous, just as
Christ is righteous.

1 John 3:7

The integrity of the upright guides them.

Proverbs 11:3

INTEGRITY

Blessed is the man who fears the LORD,
  who finds great delight in his commands.
His children will be mighty in the land;
  the generation of the upright will be blessed.
Wealth and riches are in his house,
  and his righteousness endures forever.
Even in darkness light dawns for the upright,
  for the gracious and compassionate and
    righteous man.
Good will come to him who is generous and
      lends freely,
  who conducts his affairs with justice.
Surely he will never be shaken;
  a righteous man will be remembered forever.
He will have no fear of bad news;
  his heart is steadfast, trusting in the LORD.
His heart is secure, he will have no fear.

Psalm 112:1–8

INTEGRITY

Who, then, is the man that fears the LORD?
    He will instruct him in the way
        chosen for him.
He will spend his days in prosperity,
    and his descendants will inherit the land.
The LORD confides in those who fear him;
    he makes his covenant known to them.

Psalm 25:12–14

Blessed is the man
    who does not walk in the counsel of the wicked
or stand in the way of sinners
    or sit in the seat of mockers.
But his delight is in the law of the LORD,
    and on his law he meditates day and night.
He is like a tree planted by streams of water,
    which yields its fruit in season
and whose leaf does not wither.
    Whatever he does prospers.

Psalm 1:1–3

INTEGRITY

The days of the blameless are known to the LORD,
and their inheritance will endure forever.

Psalm 37:18

Those who have served well gain an excellent
standing and great assurance in their faith in
Christ Jesus.

1 Timothy 3:13

The prayer of a righteous man is powerful
and effective.

James 5:16

I have fought the good fight, I have finished the
race, I have kept the faith. Now there is in store
for me the crown of righteousness, which the
Lord, the righteous Judge, will award to me on
that day—and not only to me, but also to all who
have longed for his appearing.

2 Timothy 4:7–8

INTEGRITY

When a man's ways are pleasing to the LORD,
he makes even his enemies live at peace
with him.

Proverbs 16:7

The world and its desires pass away, but the man
who does the will of God lives forever.

1 John 2:17

God "will give to each person according to what
he has done." To those who by persistence in
doing good seek glory, honor and immortality, he
will give eternal life.

Romans 2:6–7

The fruit of righteousness will be peace;
the effect of righteousness will be quietness and
confidence forever.

Isaiah 32:17

INTEGRITY

A man reaps what he sows. The one who sows to
please his sinful nature, from that nature will reap
destruction; the one who sows to please the Spirit,
from the Spirit will reap eternal life.

Galatians 6:7–8

Let love and faithfulness never leave you;
    bind them around your neck,
    write them on the tablet of your heart.
Then you will win favor and a good name
    in the sight of God and man.

Proverbs 3:3–4

The eyes of the Lord are on the righteous and his
ears are attentive to their prayer.

1 Peter 3:12

The LORD delights in men who are truthful.

Proverbs 12:22

INTEGRITY

The LORD takes the upright into his confidence.

Proverbs 3:32

A good name is more desirable than great riches;
    to be esteemed is better than silver or gold.

Proverbs 22:1

**May God himself, the God of peace, sanctify
you through and through. May your whole
spirit, soul and body be kept blameless at the
coming of our Lord Jesus Christ. The one who
calls you is faithful and he will do it.**

1 Thessalonians 5:23–24

Reflections on
INTEGRITY

_____

_____

_____

_____

_____

_____

_____

_____

_____

_____

_____

_____

_____

_____

_____

JOY

A voice of one calling:
"In the desert prepare
   the way for the LORD;
make straight in the wilderness
   a highway for our God.
Every valley shall be raised up,
   every mountain and hill made low;
the rough ground shall become level,
   the rugged places a plain.
And the glory of the LORD will be revealed,
   and all mankind together will see it.
   For the mouth of the LORD has spoken."

Isaiah 40:3–5

JOY

Jesus said, "As the Father has loved me, so have I loved you. Now remain in my love. If you obey my commands, you will remain in my love, just as I have obeyed my Father's commands and remain in his love. I have told you this so that my joy may be in you and that your joy may be complete."

John 15:9–11

Jesus told his disciples, "You will grieve, but your grief will turn to joy. A woman giving birth to a child has pain because her time has come; but when her baby is born she forgets the anguish because of her joy that a child is born into the world. So with you: Now is your time of grief, but I will see you again and you will rejoice, and no one will take away your joy."

John 16:20–22

JOY

The Lord is the Spirit, and where the Spirit of the
Lord is, there is freedom.

2 Corinthians 3:17

You will go out in joy
   and be led forth in peace;
the mountains and hills
   will burst into song before you,
and all the trees of the field
   will clap their hands.
Instead of the thornbush will grow the pine tree,
   and instead of briers the myrtle will grow.

Isaiah 55:12–13

A cheerful look brings joy to the heart,
   and good news gives health to the bones.

Proverbs 15:30

JOY

The prospect of the righteous is joy.

Proverbs 10:28

Though you have not seen Jesus, you love him;
and even though you do not see him now, you
believe in him and are filled with an inexpressible
and glorious joy, for you are receiving the goal of
your faith, the salvation of your souls.

1 Peter 1:8–9

A happy heart makes the face cheerful.

Proverbs 15:13

A cheerful heart is good medicine.

Proverbs 17:22

A man finds joy in giving an apt reply—
and how good is a timely word!

Proverbs 15:23

JOY

"[My people] will rejoice in their inheritance . . .
and everlasting joy will be theirs,"
declares the LORD.

Isaiah 61:7

The ransomed of the LORD will return.
They will enter Zion with singing;
everlasting joy will crown their heads.
Gladness and joy will overtake them,
and sorrow and sighing will flee away.

Isaiah 51:11

In the presence of the LORD your God, you and
your families shall eat and shall rejoice in
everything you have put your hand to, because the
LORD your God has blessed you.

Deuteronomy 12:7

JOY

Jesus said, "Ask and you will receive, and your joy
will be complete."

John 16:24

The joy of the LORD is your strength.

Nehemiah 8:10

You have made known to me the path of life,
    O LORD;
    you will fill me with joy in your presence,
with eternal pleasures at your right hand.

Psalm 16:11

You turned my wailing into dancing, O LORD;
    you removed my sackcloth and clothed me
        with joy,
that my heart may sing to you and not be silent.
    O LORD my God, I will give you thanks
        forever.

Psalm 30:11–12

JOY

Those living far away fear your wonders, O Lord;
     where morning dawns and evening fades
     you call forth songs of joy.
You care for the land and water it;
     you enrich it abundantly.
The streams of God are filled with water
     to provide the people with grain,
     for so you have ordained it.
You drench its furrows
     and level its ridges;
you soften it with showers
     and bless its crops.
You crown the year with your bounty,
     and your carts overflow with abundance.
The grasslands of the desert overflow;
     the hills are clothed with gladness.
The meadows are covered with flocks
     and the valleys are mantled with grain;
     they shout for joy and sing.

Psalm 65:8–13

JOY

When anxiety was great within me,
   your consolation brought joy to my soul,
      O Lord.

Psalm 94:19

Light is shed upon the righteous
   and joy on the upright in heart.

Psalm 97:11

The LORD has done great things for us,
   and we are filled with joy.

Psalm 126:3

Those who sow in tears
   will reap with songs of joy.
He who goes out weeping,
   carrying seed to sow,
will return with songs of joy,
   carrying sheaves with him.

Psalm 126:5–6

JOY

There is . . . joy for those who promote peace.

Proverbs 12:20

The LORD your God is with you,
   he is mighty to save.
He will take great delight in you,
   he will quiet you with his love,
   he will rejoice over you with singing.

Zephaniah 3:17

**Satisfy us in the morning with your unfailing
    love, O LORD,
    that we may sing for joy and be glad all
      our days.**

Psalm 90:14

Reflections on
JOY

_____

_____

_____

_____

_____

_____

_____

_____

_____

_____

_____

_____

_____

_____

_____

_____

LEADERSHIP

When one rules over men in righteousness,
   when he rules in the fear of God,
he is like the light of morning at sunrise
   on a cloudless morning,
like the brightness after rain
   that brings the grass from the earth.

2 Samuel 23:3–4

"I, wisdom, dwell together with prudence;
   I possess knowledge and discretion. . . .
Counsel and sound judgment are mine;
   I have understanding and power.
By me kings reign
   and rulers make laws that are just;
by me princes govern,
   and all nobles who rule on earth."

Proverbs 8:12, 14–16

LEADERSHIP

Be shepherds of God's flock that is under your care, serving as overseers—not because you must, but because you are willing, as God wants you to be; not greedy for money, but eager to serve; not lording it over those entrusted to you, but being examples to the flock. And when the Chief Shepherd appears, you will receive the crown of glory that will never fade away.

1 Peter 5:2–4

In Christ all the fullness of the Deity lives in bodily form, and you have been given fullness in Christ, who is the head over every power and authority.

Colossians 2:9–10

LEADERSHIP

Jesus knew that the Father had put all things under his power, and that he had come from God and was returning to God; so he ... poured water into a basin and began to wash his disciples' feet, drying them with the towel that was wrapped around him. ...

When Jesus had finished washing their feet, he put on his clothes and returned to his place. "Do you understand what I have done for you?" he asked them. "You call me 'Teacher' and 'Lord,' and rightly so, for that is what I am. Now that I, your Lord and Teacher, have washed your feet, you also should wash one another's feet. I have set you an example that you should do as I have done for you. ... Now that you know these things, you will be blessed if you do them."

John 13:3–5, 12–15, 17

LEADERSHIP

Jesus said, "All authority in heaven and on earth has been given to me. Therefore go and make disciples of all nations, baptizing them in the name of the Father and of the Son and of the Holy Spirit, and teaching them to obey everything I have commanded you. And surely I am with you always, to the very end of the age."

Matthew 28:18–20

You will receive power when the Holy Spirit comes on you.

Acts 1:8

LORD God, Give me wisdom and knowledge, that I may lead.

2 Chronicles 1:10

Reflections on
LEADERSHIP

_____

_____

_____

_____

_____

_____

_____

_____

_____

_____

_____

_____

_____

_____

_____

MARRIAGE

The LORD God said, "It is not good for the man to be alone. I will make a helper suitable for him."

Genesis 2:18

At the beginning of creation God "made them male and female." "For this reason a man will leave his father and mother and be united to his wife, and the two will become one flesh." So they are no longer two, but one.

Mark 10:6–8

Love is patient, love is kind. It does not envy, it does not boast, it is not proud. It is not rude, it is not self-seeking, it is not easily angered, it keeps no record of wrongs. Love does not delight in evil but rejoices with the truth. It always protects, always trusts, always hopes, always perseveres. Love never fails.

1 Corinthians 13:4–8

MARRIAGE

He who finds a wife finds what is good
   and receives favor from the LORD.

Proverbs 18:22

We know and rely on the love God has for us.
God is love. Whoever lives in love lives in God,
and God in him.

1 John 4:16

Husbands, love your wives, just as Christ loved
the church and gave himself up for her to make
her holy, cleansing her by the washing with water
through the word, and to present her to himself
as a radiant church, without stain or wrinkle or
any other blemish, but holy and blameless.
In this same way, husbands ought to love their
wives as their own bodies. He who loves his
wife loves himself.

Ephesians 5:25–28

MARRIAGE

Above all, love each other deeply, because love covers over a multitude of sins.

1 Peter 4:8

Love burns like blazing fire,
 like a mighty flame.
Many waters cannot quench love;
 rivers cannot wash it away.

Song of Songs 8:6–7

No one has ever seen God; but if we love one another, God lives in us and his love is made complete in us. We know that we live in him and he in us, because he has given us of his Spirit.

1 John 4:12–13

Houses and wealth are inherited from parents,
 but a prudent wife is from the LORD.

Proverbs 19:14

MARRIAGE

There is no fear in love. But perfect love drives
out fear.

1 John 4:18

May the Lord make your love increase and
overflow for each other.

1 Thessalonians 3:12

A wife of noble character who can find?
    She is worth far more than rubies.
Her husband has full confidence in her
    and lacks nothing of value.

Proverbs 31:10–11

MARRIAGE

A wife of noble character is her husband's crown.

Proverbs 12:4

Your wife will be like a fruitful vine
    within your house;
your sons will be like olive shoots
    around your table.
Thus is the man blessed
    who fears the LORD.

Psalm 128:3–4

**May your fountain be blessed,
    and may you rejoice in the wife of
        your youth....
May you ever be captivated by her love.**

Proverbs 5:18–19

Reflections on
MARRIAGE

_____

_____

_____

_____

_____

_____

_____

_____

_____

_____

_____

_____

_____

_____

_____

_____

OBEDIENCE

"If you do away with the yoke of oppression,
    with the pointing finger and malicious talk,
and if you spend yourselves in behalf of the hungry
    and satisfy the needs of the oppressed,
then your light will rise in the darkness,
    and your night will become like the noonday.
The LORD will guide you always;
    he will satisfy your needs in a sun-scorched land
    and will strengthen your frame.
You will be like a well-watered garden,
    like a spring whose waters never fail,"
        declares the LORD.

Isaiah 58:9–11

Give, and it will be given to you. A good measure,
pressed down, shaken together and running over,
will be poured into your lap. For with the measure
you use, it will be measured to you.

Luke 6:38

OBEDIENCE

When the Son of Man comes in his glory, and all
the angels with him, he will sit on his throne in
heavenly glory. All the nations will be gathered
before him. ... Then the King will say to those
on his right, "Come, you who are blessed by
my Father; take your inheritance, the kingdom
prepared for you since the creation of the world.
For I was hungry and you gave me something to
eat, I was thirsty and you gave me something to
drink, I was a stranger and you invited me in." ...

Then the righteous will answer him, "Lord,
when did we see you hungry and feed you, or
thirsty and give you something to drink? When
did we see you a stranger and invite you in?" ...

The King will reply, "I tell you the truth,
whatever you did for one of the least of these
brothers of mine, you did for me."

Matthew 25:31–32, 34–35, 37-38, 40

OBEDIENCE

He who is kind to the poor lends to the LORD,
and he will reward him for what he has done.

Proverbs 19:17

The Son of Man is going to come in his Father's
glory with his angels, and then he will reward each
person according to what he has done.

Matthew 16:27

Love your enemies, do good to them, and lend to
them without expecting to get anything back.
Then your reward will be great, and you will be
sons of the Most High.

Luke 6:35

Jesus said, "Behold, I am coming soon! My reward
is with me, and I will give to everyone according
to what he has done. I am the Alpha and the
Omega, the First and the Last, the Beginning and
the End."

Revelation 22:12–13

OBEDIENCE

Do you not know that in a race all the runners run, but only one gets the prize? Run in such a way as to get the prize. Everyone who competes in the games goes into strict training. They do it to get a crown that will not last; but we do it to get a crown that will last forever.

1 Corinthians 9:24–25

Jesus said, "Be faithful ... and I will give you the crown of life."

Revelation 2:10

"I will give you a new heart and put a new spirit in you; I will remove from you your heart of stone and give you a heart of flesh. And I will put my Spirit in you and move you to follow my decrees and be careful to keep my laws," declares the LORD.

Ezekiel 36:26–27

OBEDIENCE

Jesus said, "Whoever has my commands and obeys them, he is the one who loves me. He who loves me will be loved by my Father, and I too will love him and show myself to him."

John 14:21

Because of the service by which you have proved yourselves, men will praise God for the obedience that accompanies your confession of the gospel of Christ, and for your generosity in sharing with them and with everyone else.

2 Corinthians 9:13

Do not let this Book of the Law depart from your mouth; meditate on it day and night, so that you may be careful to do everything written in it. Then you will be prosperous and successful.

Joshua 1:8

OBEDIENCE

All these blessings will come upon you and
accompany you if you obey the LORD your God:
>   You will be blessed in the city and blessed in
>   the country.
>   The fruit of your womb will be blessed, and
>   the crops of your land and the young of
>   your livestock—the calves of your herds
>   and the lambs of your flocks.
>   Your basket and your kneading trough will
>   be blessed.
>   You will be blessed when you come in and
>   blessed when you go out.

Deuteronomy 28:2–6

If anyone obeys his word, God's love is truly made
complete in him.

1 John 2:5

Do not forget to do good and to share with
others, for with such sacrifices God is pleased.

Hebrews 13:16

OBEDIENCE

All the ways of the LORD are loving and faithful
for those who keep the demands
of his covenant.

Psalm 25:10

Whoever of you loves life
and desires to see many good days,
keep your tongue from evil
and your lips from speaking lies.
Turn from evil and do good;
seek peace and pursue it.

Psalm 34:12–14

Sow for yourselves righteousness,
reap the fruit of unfailing love,
and break up your unplowed ground;
for it is time to seek the LORD,
until he comes
and showers righteousness on you.

Hosea 10:12

OBEDIENCE

The Lord will richly bless you, if only you fully obey the LORD your God.

Deuteronomy 15:4–5

Jesus said, "You are my friends if you do what I command. I no longer call you servants, because a servant does not know his master's business. Instead, I have called you friends, for everything that I learned from my Father I have made known to you."

John 15:14–15

He who obeys instructions guards his life.

Proverbs 19:16

Jesus said, "If anyone loves me, he will obey my teaching. My Father will love him, and we will come to him and make our home with him."

John 14:23

OBEDIENCE

We constantly pray for you, that our God may count you worthy of his calling, and that by his power he may fulfill every good purpose of yours and every act prompted by your faith. We pray this so that the name of our Lord Jesus may be glorified in you, and you in him, according to the grace of our God and the Lord Jesus Christ.

2 Thessalonians 1:11–12

Reflections on
OBEDIENCE

_____

_____

_____

_____

_____

_____

_____

_____

_____

_____

_____

_____

_____

_____

_____

PATIENCE

The LORD is good to those whose hope is in him,
    to the one who seeks him;
it is good to wait quietly
    for the salvation of the LORD.

Lamentations 3:25–26

See how the farmer waits for the land to yield its
valuable crop and how patient he is for the
autumn and spring rains. You too, be patient and
stand firm, because the Lord's coming is near.

James 5:7–8

A man's wisdom gives him patience;
    it is to his glory to overlook an offense.

Proverbs 19:11

PATIENCE

I waited patiently for the LORD;
   he turned to me and heard my cry.
He lifted me out of the slimy pit,
   out of the mud and mire;
he set my feet on a rock
   and gave me a firm place to stand.

Psalm 40:1–2

A patient man has great understanding.

Proverbs 14:29

Wait till the Lord comes. He will bring to light
what is hidden in darkness and will expose the
motives of men's hearts. At that time each will
receive his praise from God.

1 Corinthians 4:5

A patient man calms a quarrel.

Proverbs 15:18

PATIENCE

Better a patient man than a warrior,
   a man who controls his temper than one who
      takes a city.

Proverbs 16:32

Wait for the LORD, and he will deliver you.

Proverbs 20:22

Through patience a ruler can be persuaded.

Proverbs 25:15

I was shown mercy so that in me, the worst of
sinners, Christ Jesus might display his unlimited
patience as an example for those who would
believe on him and receive eternal life.

1 Timothy 1:16

PATIENCE

The Lord is not slow in keeping his promise, as
some understand slowness. He is patient with
you, not wanting anyone to perish, but everyone
to come to repentance. ... Bear in mind that our
Lord's patience means salvation.

2 Peter 3:9, 15

Jesus said, "Since you have kept my command to
endure patiently, I will also keep you from the
hour of trial that is going to come upon the whole
world to test those who live on the earth. I am
coming soon. Hold on to what you have, so that
no one will take your crown. Him who overcomes
I will make a pillar in the temple of my God."

Revelation 3:10–12

PATIENCE

We have not stopped praying for you and
asking God to fill you with the knowledge of
his will through all spiritual wisdom and
understanding. And we pray this in order that
you may live a life worthy of the Lord and may
please him in every way: bearing fruit in every
good work, growing in the knowledge of God,
being strengthened with all power according to
his glorious might so that you may have great
endurance and patience.

Colossians 1:9–11

Reflections on
PATIENCE

_____

_____

_____

_____

_____

_____

_____

_____

_____

_____

_____

_____

_____

_____

_____

_____

PEACE

"I will grant peace in the land, and you will
lie down and no one will make you afraid,"
says the Lord.

Leviticus 26:6

I will lie down and sleep in peace,
    for you alone, O LORD,
      make me dwell in safety.

Psalm 4:8

The LORD gives strength to his people;
    the LORD blesses his people with peace.

Psalm 29:11

Great peace have they who love your law, O Lord,
    and nothing can make them stumble.

Psalm 119:165

There is ... joy for those who promote peace.

Proverbs 12:20

PEACE

A heart at peace gives life to the body.

Proverbs 14:30

You will keep in perfect peace
    him whose mind is steadfast,
    because he trusts in you, O Lord.

Isaiah 26:3

The fruit of righteousness will be peace;
    the effect of righteousness will be quietness and
        confidence forever.

Isaiah 32:17

"Though the mountains be shaken
    and the hills be removed,
yet my unfailing love for you will not be shaken
    nor my covenant of peace be removed,"
    says the LORD, who has compassion on you.

Isaiah 54:10

PEACE

All your sons will be taught by the LORD,
and great will be your children's peace.

Isaiah 54:13

You will go out in joy
and be led forth in peace;
the mountains and hills
will burst into song before you,
and all the trees of the field
will clap their hands.

Isaiah 55:12

"I will heal my people and will let them enjoy
abundant peace and security," says the Lord.

Jeremiah 33:6

LORD, you establish peace for us;
all that we have accomplished you have done
for us.

Isaiah 26:12

PEACE

Jesus said, "Peace I leave with you; my peace
I give you. I do not give to you as the world gives.
Do not let your hearts be troubled and do not
be afraid."

John 14:27

In Christ Jesus you who once were far away have
been brought near through the blood of Christ.
For he himself is our peace, who has made the two
one and has destroyed the barrier, the dividing
wall of hostility, by abolishing in his flesh the law
with its commandments and regulations. His
purpose was to create in himself one new man out
of the two, thus making peace, and in this one
body to reconcile both of them to God through
the cross, by which he put to death their hostility.
He came and preached peace to you who were far
away and peace to those who were near.

Ephesians 2:13–17

PEACE

Since we have been justified through faith,
we have peace with God through our Lord
Jesus Christ.

Romans 5:1

God was pleased to have all his fullness dwell in
Christ, and through him to reconcile to himself
all things, whether things on earth or things in
heaven, by making peace through his blood, shed
on the cross.

Colossians 1:19–20

Grace, mercy and peace from God the Father and
from Jesus Christ, the Father's Son, will be with us
in truth and love.

2 John 1:3

**May the Lord of peace himself give you peace
at all times and in every way.**

2 Thessalonians 3:16

Reflections on
PEACE

_____

_____

_____

_____

_____

_____

_____

_____

_____

_____

_____

_____

_____

_____

_____

PERSEVERANCE

Do not throw away your confidence; it will be richly rewarded. You need to persevere so that when you have done the will of God, you will receive what he has promised.

Hebrews 10:35–36

Blessed is the man who perseveres under trial, because when he has stood the test, he will receive the crown of life that God has promised to those who love him.

James 1:12

Our present sufferings are not worth comparing with the glory that will be revealed in us.

Romans 8:18

PERSEVERANCE

Since we are surrounded by such a great cloud of witnesses, let us throw off everything that hinders and the sin that so easily entangles, and let us run with perseverance the race marked out for us. Let us fix our eyes on Jesus, the author and perfecter of our faith, who for the joy set before him endured the cross, scorning its shame, and sat down at the right hand of the throne of God. Consider him who endured such opposition from sinful men, so that you will not grow weary and lose heart.

Hebrews 12:1–3

Our salvation is nearer now than when we first believed. The night is nearly over; the day is almost here.

Romans 13:11–12

God who began a good work in you will carry it on to completion until the day of Christ Jesus.

Philippians 1:6

PERSEVERANCE

Our light and momentary troubles are achieving
for us an eternal glory that far outweighs them all.

2 Corinthians 4:17

The world and its desires pass away, but the man
who does the will of God lives forever.

1 John 2:17

Jesus said: "It is done. I am the Alpha and the
Omega, the Beginning and the End. To him who
is thirsty I will give to drink without cost from the
spring of the water of life. He who overcomes will
inherit all this, and I will be his God and he will
be my son."

Revelation 21:6–7

Let us not become weary in doing good, for at the
proper time we will reap a harvest if we do not
give up.

Galatians 6:9

PERSEVERANCE

We know that suffering produces perseverance;
perseverance, character; and character, hope.

Romans 5:3–4

Watch your life and doctrine closely. Persevere in
them, because if you do, you will save both
yourself and your hearers.

1 Timothy 4:16

For a little while you may have had to suffer grief
in all kinds of trials. These have come so that your
faith—of greater worth than gold, which perishes
even though refined by fire—may be proved
genuine and may result in praise, glory and honor
when Jesus Christ is revealed.

1 Peter 1:6–7

Be strong and do not give up, for your work will
be rewarded.

2 Chronicles 15:7

PERSEVERANCE

Consider it pure joy, my brothers, whenever you
face trials of many kinds, because you know that
the testing of your faith develops perseverance.
Perseverance must finish its work so that you may
be mature and complete, not lacking anything.

James 1:2–4

He who stands firm to the end will be saved.

Matthew 10:22

If we died with Christ,
    we will also live with him;
if we endure,
    we will also reign with him.

2 Timothy 2:11–12

If you suffer for doing good and you endure it,
this is commendable before God.

1 Peter 2:20

PERSEVERANCE

God knows the way that I take;
> when he has tested me, I will come forth
> > as gold.

Job 23:10

If you are insulted because of the name of Christ,
you are blessed, for the Spirit of glory and of God
rests on you.

1 Peter 4:14

Jesus said,
"Blessed are you when men hate you,
> when they exclude you and insult you
> and reject your name as evil,
> because of the Son of Man.
"Rejoice in that day and leap for joy, because great
is your reward in heaven."

Luke 6:22–23

PERSEVERANCE

Forgetting what is behind and straining toward
what is ahead, I press on toward the goal to win
the prize for which God has called me heavenward
in Christ Jesus.

Philippians 3:13–14

**May the Lord direct your hearts into God's love
and Christ's perseverance.**

2 Thessalonians 3:5

Reflections on
PERSEVERANCE

_____

_____

_____

_____

_____

_____

_____

_____

_____

_____

_____

_____

_____

_____

_____

_____

_____

POWER

Jesus said, "You will receive power when the Holy Spirit comes on you."

Acts 1:8

God's divine power has given us everything we need for life and godliness through our knowledge of him who called us by his own glory and goodness.

2 Peter 1:3

God did not give us a spirit of timidity, but a spirit of power, of love and of self-discipline.

2 Timothy 1:7

Jesus said, "My grace is sufficient for you, for my power is made perfect in weakness."

2 Corinthians 12:9

POWER

We pray ... that you may live a life worthy of the
Lord and may please him in every way: bearing
fruit in every good work, growing in the knowledge of God, being strengthened with all power
according to his glorious might so that you may
have great endurance and patience.

Colossians 1:10–11

I pray . . . that the eyes of your heart may be
enlightened in order that you may know the
hope to which God has called you, the riches of
his glorious inheritance in the saints, and his
incomparably great power for us who believe.
That power is like the working of his mighty
strength, which he exerted in Christ when he
raised him from the dead.

Ephesians 1:18–20

POWER

By his power God raised the Lord from the dead, and he will raise us also.

1 Corinthians 6:14

We ... pray ... that our God may count you worthy of his calling, and that by his power he may fulfill every good purpose of yours and every act prompted by your faith.

2 Thessalonians 1:11

You are the God who performs miracles;
    you display your power among the peoples.
With your mighty arm you redeemed
        your people.

Psalm 77:14–15

The weapons we fight with are not the weapons of the world. On the contrary, they have divine power to demolish strongholds.

2 Corinthians 10:4

POWER

God gives strength to the weary
and increases the power of the weak.
Even youths grow tired and weary,
and young men stumble and fall;
but those who hope in the LORD
will renew their strength.
They will soar on wings like eagles;
they will run and not grow weary,
they will walk and not be faint.

Isaiah 40:29–31

You are awesome, O God, in your sanctuary;
the God of Israel gives power and strength to
his people.

Psalm 68:35

POWER

I know that the LORD saves his anointed;
  he answers him from his holy heaven
  with the saving power of his right hand.

Psalm 20:6

**I want to know Christ and the power of his
resurrection and the fellowship of sharing in
his sufferings, becoming like him in his death,
and so, somehow, to attain to the resurrection
from the dead.**

Philippians 3:10–11

Reflections on
POWER

_____

_____

_____

_____

_____

_____

_____

_____

_____

_____

_____

_____

_____

_____

_____

_____

_____

PRAYER

The LORD ... hears the prayer of the righteous.

Proverbs 15:29

The prayer of a righteous man is powerful
and effective.

James 5:16

Jesus said, "When you pray, do not be like the
hypocrites, for they love to pray standing in the
synagogues and on the street corners to be seen by
men. I tell you the truth, they have received their
reward in full. But when you pray, go into your
room, close the door and pray to your Father, who
is unseen. Then your Father, who sees what is
done in secret, will reward you."

Matthew 6:5–6

PRAYER

Our Father in heaven,
hallowed be your name,
your kingdom come,
your will be done
   on earth as it is in heaven.
Give us today our daily bread.
Forgive us our debts,
   as we also have forgiven our debtors.
And lead us not into temptation,
but deliver us from the evil one.

Matthew 6:9–13

Christ Jesus, who died—more than that, who was
raised to life—is at the right hand of God and is
also interceding for us.

Romans 8:34

PRAYER

The Spirit helps us in our weakness. We do not
know what we ought to pray for, but the Spirit
himself intercedes for us with groans that words
cannot express. And he who searches our hearts
knows the mind of the Spirit, because the Spirit
intercedes for the saints in accordance with
God's will.

Romans 8:26–27

Because Jesus lives forever, he has a permanent
priesthood. Therefore he is able to save completely
those who come to God through him, because he
always lives to intercede for them.

Hebrews 7:24–25

Prayer

Since we have a great high priest who has gone
through the heavens, Jesus the Son of God, let us
hold firmly to the faith we profess. For we do
not have a high priest who is unable to
sympathize with our weaknesses, but we have
one who has been tempted in every way, just as
we are—yet was without sin. Let us then
approach the throne of grace with confidence, so
that we may receive mercy and find grace to help
us in our time of need.

Hebrews 4:14–16

Jesus said, "I will do whatever you ask in my
name, so that the Son may bring glory to the
Father. You may ask me for anything in my name,
and I will do it."

John 14:13–14

If you believe, you will receive whatever you ask
for in prayer.

Matthew 21:22

PRAYER

Jesus said, "If two of you on earth agree about anything you ask for, it will be done for you by my Father in heaven."

Matthew 18:19

The prayer offered in faith will make the sick person well; the Lord will raise him up. If he has sinned, he will be forgiven.

James 5:15

Whatever you ask for in prayer, believe that you have received it, and it will be yours.

Mark 11:24

This is the confidence we have in approaching God: that if we ask anything according to his will, he hears us. And if we know that he hears us— whatever we ask—we know that we have what we asked of him.

1 John 5:14–15

PRAYER

In Christ and through faith in him we may
approach God with freedom and confidence.

Ephesians 3:12

The prayer of the upright pleases the LORD.

Proverbs 15:8

The LORD has heard my cry for mercy;
   the LORD accepts my prayer.

Psalm 6:9

In my distress I called to the LORD;
   I called out to my God.
From his temple he heard my voice;
   my cry came to his ears.

2 Samuel 22:7

PRAYER

The eyes of the Lord are on the righteous and his ears are attentive to their prayer.

1 Peter 3:12

I urge ... that requests, prayers, intercession and thanksgiving be made for everyone—for kings and all those in authority, that we may live peaceful and quiet lives in all godliness and holiness.

1 Timothy 2:1–2

Do not be anxious about anything, but in everything, by prayer and petition, with thanksgiving, present your requests to God. And the peace of God, which transcends all understanding, will guard your hearts and your minds in Christ Jesus.

Philippians 4:6–7

PRAYER

Jesus said, "Love your enemies and pray for those
who persecute you, that you may be sons of your
Father in heaven."

Matthew 5:44–45

"You will call upon me and come and pray to me,
and I will listen to you. You will seek me and find
me when you seek me with all your heart. I will
be found by you," declares the LORD.

Jeremiah 29:12–14

Let everyone who is godly pray to you, Lord,
    while you may be found;
surely when the mighty waters rise,
    they will not reach him.

Psalm 32:6

PRAYER

Know that the LORD has set apart
    the godly for himself;
  the LORD will hear when I call to him.

Psalm 4:3

This poor man called, and the LORD heard him;
  he saved him out of all his troubles.

Psalm 34:6

God will respond to the prayer of the destitute;
  he will not despise their plea.

Psalm 102:17

**In the day of my trouble I will call to you,
    O LORD,
  for you will answer me.**

Psalm 86:7

Reflections on
PRAYER

_____

_____

_____

_____

_____

_____

_____

_____

_____

_____

_____

_____

_____

_____

_____

PRESENCE OF GOD

"My Presence will go with you, and I will give you rest," says the Lord.

Exodus 33:14

Jesus said, "All authority in heaven and on earth has been given to me. Therefore go and make disciples of all nations, baptizing them in the name of the Father and of the Son and of the Holy Spirit, and teaching them to obey everything I have commanded you. And surely I am with you always, to the very end of the age."

Matthew 28:18–20

"You will seek me and find me when you seek me with all your heart. I will be found by you," declares the LORD.

Jeremiah 29:13–14

Come near to God and he will come near to you.

James 4:8

PRESENCE OF GOD

The eyes of the LORD are on the righteous
and his ears are attentive to their cry.

Psalm 34:15

O LORD, where can I go from your Spirit?
Where can I flee from your presence?
If I go up to the heavens, you are there;
if I make my bed in the depths, you are there.
If I rise on the wings of the dawn,
if I settle on the far side of the sea,
even there your hand will guide me,
your right hand will hold me fast.

Psalm 139:7–10

The LORD will hear when I call to him.

Psalm 4:3

God is present in the company of the righteous.

Psalm 14:5

PRESENCE OF GOD

Jesus said, "Where two or three come together in my name, there am I with them."

Matthew 18:20

"Before they call I will answer;
   while they are still speaking I will hear,"
      says the LORD.

Isaiah 65:24

If ... you seek the LORD your God, you will find him if you look for him with all your heart and with all your soul.

Deuteronomy 4:29

"I am bringing my righteousness near,
   it is not far away,"
      declares the LORD.

Isaiah 46:13

PRESENCE OF GOD

The God of love and peace will be with you.

2 Corinthians 13:11

The LORD is near to all who call on him,
to all who call on him in truth.

Psalm 145:18

The virgin will be with child and will give birth to
a son, and they will call him Immanuel—which
means, "God with us."

Matthew 1:23

The Word became flesh and made his dwelling
among us. We have seen his glory, the glory of the
One and Only, who came from the Father, full of
grace and truth.

John 1:14

PRESENCE OF GOD

Let us acknowledge the LORD;
  let us press on to acknowledge him.
As surely as the sun rises,
  he will appear;
he will come to us like the winter rains,
  like the spring rains that water the earth.

Hosea 6:3

Arise, shine, for your light has come,
  and the glory of the LORD rises upon you.
See, darkness covers the earth
  and thick darkness is over the peoples,
but the LORD rises upon you
  and his glory appears over you.

Isaiah 60:1–2

The kingdom of heaven is near.

Matthew 4:17

PRESENCE OF GOD

The people walking in darkness
    have seen a great light;
on those living in the land of the shadow of death
    a light has dawned.

Isaiah 9:2

The LORD your God goes with you; he will never
leave you nor forsake you.

Deuteronomy 31:6

The glory of the LORD fills the whole earth.

Numbers 14:21

**May the grace of the Lord Jesus Christ, and the
love of God, and the fellowship of the Holy
Spirit be with you.**

2 Corinthians 13:14

Reflections on the
PRESENCE OF GOD

_____

_____

_____

_____

_____

_____

_____

_____

_____

_____

_____

_____

_____

_____

_____

_____

PRIORITIES

There is a time for everything,
   and a season for every activity under heaven:
   a time to be born and a time to die,
   a time to plant and a time to uproot,
   a time to kill and a time to heal,
   a time to tear down and a time to build,
   a time to weep and a time to laugh,
   a time to mourn and a time to dance,
   a time to scatter stones and a time
     to gather them,
   a time to embrace and a time to refrain,
   a time to search and a time to give up,
   a time to keep and a time to throw away,
   a time to tear and a time to mend,
   a time to be silent and a time to speak,
   a time to love and a time to hate,
   a time for war and a time for peace. ...
God has made everything beautiful in its time.

Ecclesiastes 3:1–8, 11

PRIORITIES

Jesus went to eat in the house of a prominent pharisee. ... When Jesus noticed how the guests picked the places of honor at the table, he told them this parable: "When someone invites you to a wedding feast, do not take the place of honor, for a person more distinguished than you may have been invited. If so, the host who invited both of you will come and say to you, 'Give this man your seat.' Then, humiliated, you will have to take the least important place. But when you are invited, take the lowest place, so that when your host comes, he will say to you, 'Friend, move up to a better place.' Then you will be honored in the presence of all your fellow guests. For everyone who exalts himself will be humbled, and he who humbles himself will be exalted."

Luke 14:1, 7–11

PRIORITIES

Jesus said, "Whoever loses his life for me will
find it."

Matthew 16:25

Better the little that the righteous have
   than the wealth of many wicked;
for the power of the wicked will be broken,
   but the LORD upholds the righteous.

Psalm 37:16–17

Better is one day in your courts
   than a thousand elsewhere, O LORD;
I would rather be a doorkeeper in the house of
      my God
   than dwell in the tents of the wicked.
For the LORD God is a sun and shield;
   the LORD bestows favor and honor;
no good thing does he withhold
   from those whose walk is blameless.

Psalm 84:10–11

PRIORITIES

Humble yourselves before the Lord, and he will lift you up.

James 4:10

Whoever trusts in his riches will fall,
   but the righteous will thrive like a green leaf.

Proverbs 11:28

Set your minds on things above, not on earthly things. For you died, and your life is now hidden with Christ in God. When Christ, who is your life, appears, then you also will appear with him in glory.

Colossians 3:2–4

Store up for yourselves treasures in heaven, where moth and rust do not destroy, and where thieves do not break in and steal. For where your treasure is, there your heart will be also.

Matthew 6:20–21

PRIORITIES

"Let not the wise man boast of his wisdom
  or the strong man boast of his strength
  or the rich man boast of his riches,
but let him who boasts boast about this:
  that he understands and knows me,
that I am the LORD, who exercises kindness,
  justice and righteousness on earth,
  for in these I delight,"
  declares the LORD.

Jeremiah 9:23–24

In view of God's mercy, . . . offer your bodies as
living sacrifices, holy and pleasing to God—this is
your spiritual act of worship. Do not conform any
longer to the pattern of this world, but be
transformed by the renewing of your mind. Then
you will be able to test and approve what God's
will is—his good, pleasing and perfect will.

Romans 12:1–2

PRIORITIES

He who sows righteousness reaps a sure reward.

Proverbs 11:18

He who pursues righteousness and love
  finds life, prosperity and honor.

Proverbs 21:21

Jesus said, "Do not worry, saying 'What shall we
eat?' or 'What shall we drink?' or 'What shall we
wear?' For ... your heavenly Father knows that
you need them. But seek first his kingdom and his
righteousness, and all these things will be given to
you as well."

Matthew 6:31–33

PRIORITIES

Humility and the fear of the LORD
  bring wealth and honor and life.

Proverbs 22:4

When you give a banquet, invite the poor, the
crippled, the lame, the blind, and you will be
blessed. Although they cannot repay you, you
will be repaid at the resurrection of the righteous.

Luke 14:13–14

**O LORD, teach us to number our days aright,
  that we may gain a heart of wisdom.**

Psalm 90:12

Reflections on
PRIORITIES

_____

_____

_____

_____

_____

_____

_____

_____

_____

_____

_____

_____

_____

_____

_____

_____

_____

PROTECTION

I lift up my eyes to the hills—
    where does my help come from?
My help comes from the LORD,
    the Maker of heaven and earth.
He will not let your foot slip—
    he who watches over you will not slumber;
indeed, he who watches over Israel
    will neither slumber nor sleep.
The LORD watches over you—
    the LORD is your shade at your right hand;
the sun will not harm you by day,
    nor the moon by night.
The LORD will keep you from all harm—
    he will watch over your life;
the LORD will watch over your coming and going
    both now and forevermore.

Psalm 121

PROTECTION

Jesus said, "Everyone who hears these words of mine and puts them into practice is like a wise man who built his house on the rock. The rain came down, the streams rose, and the winds blew and beat against that house; yet it did not fall, because it had its foundation on the rock."

Matthew 7:24–25

This is what the LORD says—
"Fear not, for I have redeemed you;
    I have summoned you by name; you are mine.
When you pass through the waters,
    I will be with you;
and when you pass through the rivers,
    they will not sweep over you.
When you walk through the fire,
    you will not be burned;
    the flames will not set you ablaze."

Isaiah 43:1–2

PROTECTION

You are my hiding place, O Lord;
    you will protect me from trouble
    and surround me with songs of deliverance.

Psalm 32:7

You are a shield around me, O LORD;
    you bestow glory on me and lift up my head.
To the LORD I cry aloud,
    and he answers me from his holy hill.

Psalm 3:3–4

From the LORD comes deliverance.

Psalm 3:8

In the day of trouble
    the LORD will keep me safe in his dwelling;
he will hide me in the shelter of his tabernacle
    and set me high upon a rock.

Psalm 27:5

PROTECTION

The righteous cry out, and the LORD hears them;
  he delivers them from all their troubles.

Psalm 34:17

Blessed is he who has regard for the weak;
  the LORD delivers him in times of trouble.
The LORD will protect him and preserve his life;
  he will bless him in the land.

Psalm 41:1–2

O my Strength, I watch for you;
  you, O God, are my fortress, my loving God.

Psalm 59:9–10

PROTECTION

The LORD will cover you with his feathers,
   and under his wings you will find refuge;
   his faithfulness will be your shield and rampart.
You will not fear the terror of night,
   nor the arrow that flies by day.

Psalm 91:4–5

If you make the Most High your dwelling—
   even the LORD, who is my refuge—
then no harm will befall you,
   no disaster will come near your tent.
For he will command his angels concerning you
   to guard you in all your ways.

Psalm 91:9–11

The Lord is faithful, and he will strengthen and
protect you from the evil one.

2 Thessalonians 3:3

PROTECTION

"Because he loves me," says the LORD, "I will
    rescue him;
  I will protect him, for he acknowledges
    my name.
He will call upon me, and I will answer him;
  I will be with him in trouble,
  I will deliver him and honor him.
With long life will I satisfy him
  and show him my salvation."

Psalm 91:14–16

The way of the LORD is a refuge for the righteous.

Proverbs 10:29

The righteous man is rescued from trouble.

Proverbs 11:8

The name of the LORD is a strong tower;
  the righteous run to it and are safe.

Proverbs 18:10

PROTECTION

Worship the LORD your God; it is he who will
deliver you.

2 Kings 17:39

The LORD guards the lives of his faithful ones.

Psalm 97:10

You are my refuge and my shield, O LORD;
I have put my hope in your word.

Psalm 119:114

O LORD, you have been a refuge for the poor,
a refuge for the needy in his distress,
a shelter from the storm
and a shade from the heat.

Isaiah 25:4

**Do not withhold your mercy from me,
O LORD;
may your love and your truth always
protect me.**

Psalm 40:11

Reflections on
PROTECTION

_____

_____

_____

_____

_____

_____

_____

_____

_____

_____

_____

_____

_____

_____

_____

_____

PROVISION

God... richly provides us with everything for
our enjoyment.

1 Timothy 6:17

Jesus said, "Why do you worry about clothes? See
how the lilies of the field grow. They do not labor
or spin. Yet I tell you that not even Solomon in all
his splendor was dressed like one of these. If that
is how God clothes the grass of the field, which is
here today and tomorrow is thrown into the fire,
will he not much more clothe you?... So do not
worry, saying, 'What shall we eat?' or 'What shall
we drink?' or 'What shall we wear?' For... your
heavenly Father knows that you need them. But
seek first his kingdom and his righteousness, and
all these things will be given to you as well."

Matthew 6:28–33

PROVISION

Remember the LORD your God, for it is he who gives you the ability to produce wealth.

Deuteronomy 8:18

You still the hunger of those you cherish,
 O LORD;
 their sons have plenty,
 and they store up wealth for their children.

Psalm 17:14

"Bring the whole tithe into the storehouse, that there may be food in my house. Test me in this," says the LORD Almighty, "and see if I will not throw open the floodgates of heaven and pour out so much blessing that you will not have room enough for it."

Malachi 3:10

PROVISION

I was young and now I am old,
  yet I have never seen the righteous forsaken
  or their children begging bread.

Psalm 37:25

Honor the LORD with your wealth,
  with the firstfruits of all your crops;
then your barns will be filled to overflowing,
  and your vats will brim over with new wine.

Proverbs 3:9–10

Fear the LORD, you his saints,
  for those who fear him lack nothing.
The lions may grow weak and hungry,
  but those who seek the LORD lack no
    good thing.

Psalm 34:9–10

PROVISION

God who did not spare his own Son, but gave him up for us all—how will he not also, along with him, graciously give us all things?

Romans 8:32

Which of you, if his son asks for bread, will give him a stone? Or if he asks for a fish, will give him a snake? If you, then, though you are evil, know how to give good gifts to your children, how much more will your Father in heaven give good gifts to those who ask him!

Matthew 7:9–11

God will meet all your needs according to his glorious riches in Christ Jesus.

Philippians 4:19

PROVISION

The eyes of all look to you, O LORD,
    and you give them their food at the proper time.
You open your hand
    and satisfy the desires of every living thing.

Psalm 145:15–16

Be glad, O people of Zion,
    rejoice in the LORD your God,
for he has given you
    the autumn rains in righteousness.
He sends you abundant showers,
    both autumn and spring rains, as before.
The threshing floors will be filled with grain;
    the vats will overflow with new wine and oil.

Joel 2:23–24

Jesus said, "Ask and you will receive, and your joy
will be complete."

John 16:24

PROVISION

The LORD will indeed give what is good.

Psalm 85:12

To God who is able to do immeasurably more than all we ask or imagine, according to his power that is at work within us, to him be glory in the church and in Christ Jesus throughout all generations, for ever and ever! Amen.

Ephesians 3:20–21

Reflections on
PROVISION

_____

_____

_____

_____

_____

_____

_____

_____

_____

_____

_____

_____

_____

_____

_____

_____

_____

REST

Stand at the crossroads and look;
   ask for the ancient paths,
ask where the good way is, and walk in it,
   and you will find rest for your souls.

Jeremiah 6:16

God grants sleep to those he loves.

Psalm 127:2

I lie down and sleep;
   I wake again, because the LORD sustains me.

Psalm 3:5

Jesus said, "Come to me, all you who are weary
and burdened, and I will give you rest. Take my
yoke upon you and learn from me, for I am gentle
and humble in heart, and you will find rest for
your souls. For my yoke is easy and my burden
is light."

Matthew 11:28–30

REST

There remains ... a Sabbath-rest for the people of God; for anyone who enters God's rest also rests from his own work, just as God did from his.

Hebrews 4:9–10

The LORD is my shepherd, I shall not be in want.
   He makes me lie down in green pastures,
he leads me beside quiet waters,
   he restores my soul.

Psalm 23:1–3

My soul finds rest in God alone;
   my salvation comes from him.
He alone is my rock and my salvation;
   he is my fortress, I will never be shaken.

Psalm 62:1–2

REST

Those who walk uprightly
enter into peace;
they find rest.

Isaiah 57:2

He who dwells in the shelter of the Most High
will rest in the shadow of the Almighty.

Psalm 91:1

I will lie down and sleep in peace,
for you alone, O LORD,
make me dwell in safety.

Psalm 4:8

REST

Preserve sound judgment and discernment,
   do not let them out of your sight;
they will be life for you,
   an ornament to grace your neck.
Then you will go on your way in safety,
   and your foot will not stumble;
when you lie down, you will not be afraid;
   when you lie down, your sleep will be sweet.

Proverbs 3:21–24

"I will refresh the weary and satisfy the faint," says
the LORD.

Jeremiah 31:25

REST

Do you not know?
Have you not heard?
The LORD is the everlasting God,
the Creator of the ends of the earth.
He will not grow tired or weary,
and his understanding no one can fathom.
He gives strength to the weary
and increases the power of the weak.
Even youths grow tired and weary,
and young men stumble and fall;
but those who hope in the LORD
will renew their strength.

Isaiah 40:28–31

REST

"My people will live in peaceful dwelling places,
    in secure homes,
        in undisturbed places of rest," says the Lord.

Isaiah 32:18

In repentance and rest is your salvation,
    in quietness and trust is your strength.

Isaiah 30:15

**Let the beloved of the LORD rest secure in him,
    for he shields him all day long,
    and the one the LORD loves rests
        between his shoulders.**

Deuteronomy 33:12

Reflections on
REST

_____

_____

_____

_____

_____

_____

_____

_____

_____

_____

_____

_____

_____

_____

_____

SALVATION

God so loved the world that he gave his one and only Son, that whoever believes in him shall not perish but have eternal life.

John 3:16

Jesus declared, "I am the bread of life. He who comes to me will never go hungry, and he who believes in me will never be thirsty."

John 6:35

Jesus said, "Here I am! I stand at the door and knock. If anyone hears my voice and opens the door, I will come in and eat with him, and he with me."

Revelation 3:20

Jesus said, "Whoever drinks the water I give him will never thirst. Indeed, the water I give him will become in him a spring of water welling up to eternal life."

John 4:14

SALVATION

If you confess with your mouth, "Jesus is Lord," and believe in your heart that God raised him from the dead, you will be saved. For it is with your heart that you believe and are justified, and it is with your mouth that you confess and are saved. As the Scripture says, "Anyone who trusts in him will never be put to shame."

Romans 10:9–11

Repent and be baptized, every one of you, in the name of Jesus Christ for the forgiveness of your sins. And you will receive the gift of the Holy Spirit. The promise is for you and your children and for all who are far off—for all whom the Lord our God will call.

Acts 2:38–39

SALVATION

You also were included in Christ when you heard the word of truth, the gospel of your salvation. Having believed, you were marked in him with a seal, the promised Holy Spirit, who is a deposit guaranteeing our inheritance until the redemption of those who are God's possession—to the praise of his glory.

Ephesians 1:13–14

Jesus said, "I am the good shepherd; I know my sheep and my sheep know me.... My sheep listen to my voice; I know them, and they follow me. I give them eternal life, and they shall never perish; no one can snatch them out of my hand. My Father, who has given them to me, is greater than all; no one can snatch them out of my Father's hand. I and the Father are one."

John 10:14, 27–30

SALVATION

The LORD redeems his servants;
> no one will be condemned who takes refuge
> > in him.

Psalm 34:22

Everyone who calls on the name of the Lord will
be saved.

Acts 2:21

There is now no condemnation for those who are
in Christ Jesus, because through Christ Jesus the
law of the Spirit of life set me free from the law of
sin and death.

Romans 8:1–2

SALVATION

Jesus said, "I am the resurrection and the life. He who believes in me will live, even though he dies; and whoever lives and believes in me will never die."

John 11:25–26

Ask and it will be given to you; seek and you will find; knock and the door will be opened to you. For everyone who asks receives; he who seeks finds; and to him who knocks, the door will be opened.

Matthew 7:7–8

The gospel ... is the power of God for the salvation of everyone who believes.

Romans 1:16

SALVATION

Jesus is able to save completely those who come to God through him.

Hebrews 7:25

Jesus said, "I tell you the truth, whoever hears my word and believes him who sent me has eternal life and will not be condemned; he has crossed over from death to life."

John 5:24

If anyone acknowledges that Jesus is the Son of God, God lives in him and he in God.

1 John 4:15

If the Son sets you free, you will be free indeed.

John 8:36

The wages of sin is death, but the gift of God is eternal life in Christ Jesus our Lord.

Romans 6:23

SALVATION

Righteousness from God comes through faith
in Jesus Christ to all who believe. There is no
difference, for all have sinned and fall short of
the glory of God, and are justified freely by his
grace through the redemption that came by
Christ Jesus.

Romans 3:22–24

If the Spirit of him who raised Jesus from the
dead is living in you, he who raised Christ from
the dead will also give life to your mortal bodies
through his Spirit, who lives in you.

Romans 8:11

God did not send his Son into the world to
condemn the world, but to save the world
through him.

John 3:17

SALVATION

Jesus is the image of the invisible God, the firstborn over all creation. For by him all things were created: things in heaven and on earth, visible and invisible, whether thrones or powers or rulers or authorities; all things were created by him and for him. He is before all things, and in him all things hold together. And he is the head of the body, the church; he is the beginning and the firstborn from among the dead, so that in everything he might have the supremacy. For God was pleased to have all his fullness dwell in him, and through him to reconcile to himself all things, whether things on earth or things in heaven, by making peace through his blood, shed on the cross.

Colossians 1:15–20

The Son of Man came to seek and to save what was lost.

Luke 19:10

SALVATION

Jesus said, "My Father's will is that everyone who looks to the Son and believes in him shall have eternal life, and I will raise him up at the last day."

John 6:40

God did not appoint us to suffer wrath but to receive salvation through our Lord Jesus Christ.

1 Thessalonians 5:9

The LORD has clothed me with
    garments of salvation
 and arrayed me in a robe of righteousness,
as a bridegroom adorns his head like a priest,
    and as a bride adorns herself with her jewels.

Isaiah 61:10

Christ loved us and gave himself up for us as a fragrant offering and sacrifice to God.

Ephesians 5:2

SALVATION

Christ was sacrificed once to take away the sins of many people; and he will appear a second time, not to bear sin, but to bring salvation to those who are waiting for him.

Hebrews 9:28

Praise be to the God and Father of our Lord Jesus Christ! In his great mercy he has given us new birth into a living hope through the resurrection of Jesus Christ from the dead, and into an inheritance that can never perish, spoil or fade—kept in heaven for you, who through faith are shielded by God's power until the coming of the salvation that is ready to be revealed in the last time.

1 Peter 1:3–5

Reflections on
SALVATION

_____

_____

_____

_____

_____

_____

_____

_____

_____

_____

_____

_____

_____

_____

_____

_____

SECURITY

"Be still, and know that I am God.

Psalm 46:10

"I know the plans I have for you," declares the LORD, "plans to prosper you and not to harm you, plans to give you hope and a future."

Jeremiah 29:11

The LORD watches over the way of the righteous.

Psalm 1:6

LORD, you have assigned me my portion and
    my cup;
  you have made my lot secure.
The boundary lines have fallen for me in
    pleasant places;
  surely I have a delightful inheritance.

Psalm 16:5–6

SECURITY

I have set the LORD always before me.
Because he is at my right hand,
I will not be shaken.
Therefore my heart is glad and my tongue rejoices;
my body also will rest secure.

Psalm 16:8–9

The LORD preserves the faithful.

Psalm 31:23

The angel of the LORD encamps around those
who fear him,
and he delivers them.

Psalm 34:7

Cast your cares on the LORD
and he will sustain you;
he will never let the righteous fall.

Psalm 55:22

SECURITY

If God is for us, who can be against us?

Romans 8:31

Jesus said, "Are not two sparrows sold for a penny?
Yet not one of them will fall to the ground apart
from the will of your Father. And even the very
hairs of your head are all numbered. So don't be
afraid; you are worth more than many sparrows."

Matthew 10:29–31

In all things God works for the good of those
who love him, who have been called according
to his purpose.

Romans 8:28

SECURITY

Jesus said, "Peace I leave with you; my peace
I give you. I do not give to you as the world gives.
Do not let your hearts be troubled and do not
be afraid."

John 14:27

Jesus said, "Do not be afraid, little flock, for your
Father has been pleased to give you the kingdom."

Luke 12:32

Jesus Christ is the same yesterday and today and
forever.

Hebrews 13:8

God does not change like shifting shadows.

James 1:17

God is light; in him there is no darkness at all.

1 John 1:5

SECURITY

The Lord will rescue me from every evil attack
and will bring me safely to his heavenly kingdom.

2 Timothy 4:18

Jesus said, "In this world you will have trouble.
But take heart! I have overcome the world."

John 16:33

Everyone born of God overcomes the world. This
is the victory that has overcome the world, even
our faith. Who is it that overcomes the world?
Only he who believes that Jesus is the Son of God.

1 John 5:4–5

SECURITY

Though I walk in the midst of trouble,
    you preserve my life;
you stretch out your hand against the anger of
            my foes,
    with your right hand you save me.
The LORD will fulfill his purpose for me;
    your love, O LORD, endures forever.

Psalm 138:7–8

Since we have been justified through faith, we
have peace with God through our Lord Jesus
Christ, through whom we have gained access by
faith into this grace in which we now stand.

Romans 5:1–2

If we live, we live to the Lord; and if we die, we
die to the Lord. So, whether we live or die, we
belong to the Lord.

Romans 14:8

SECURITY

Our citizenship is in heaven. And we eagerly await
a Savior from there, the Lord Jesus Christ, who,
by the power that enables him to bring everything
under his control, will transform our lowly bodies
so that they will be like his glorious body.

Philippians 3:20–21

No matter how many promises God has made,
they are "Yes" in Christ.

2 Corinthians 1:20

It is God who makes ... you stand firm in Christ.
He anointed us, set his seal of ownership on us,
and put his Spirit in our hearts as a deposit,
guaranteeing what is to come.

2 Corinthians 1:21–22

SECURITY

The eternal God is your refuge,
    and underneath are the everlasting arms.

Deuteronomy 33:27

Everything God does will endure forever; nothing
can be added to it and nothing taken from it.

Ecclesiastes 3:14

"Even to your old age and gray hairs
    I am he, I am he who will sustain you.
I have made you and I will carry you;
    I will sustain you and I will rescue you,"
        declares the LORD.

Isaiah 46:4

God's solid foundation stands firm, sealed with
this inscription: "The Lord knows those who
are his."

2 Timothy 2:19

SECURITY

"My salvation will last forever,
   my righteousness will never fail,"
      declares the LORD.

Isaiah 51:6

I lie down and sleep;
   I wake again, because the LORD sustains me.

Psalm 3:5

As long as the earth endures,
seedtime and harvest,
cold and heat,
summer and winter,
day and night
will never cease.

Genesis 8:22

SECURITY

The works of God's hands are faithful and just;
    all his precepts are trustworthy.
They are steadfast for ever and ever,
    done in faithfulness and uprightness.
He provided redemption for his people;
    he ordained his covenant forever—
holy and awesome is his name.

Psalm 111:7–9

You have been my refuge, O LORD,
    a strong tower against the foe.
I long to dwell in your tent forever
    and take refuge in the shelter of your wings.

Psalm 61:3

God makes my feet like the feet of a deer;
    he enables me to stand on the heights.

2 Samuel 22:34

SECURITY

You broaden the path beneath me, O LORD,
 so that my ankles do not turn.

2 Samuel 22:37

"I will heal my people and will let them enjoy
abundant peace and security," declares the LORD.

Jeremiah 33:6

The LORD is faithful to all his promises
 and loving toward all he has made.

Psalm 145:13

There is no wisdom, no insight, no plan
 that can succeed against the LORD.

Proverbs 21:30

We have one who speaks to the Father in our
defense—Jesus Christ, the Righteous One.

1 John 2:1

SECURITY

"As the rain and the snow
   come down from heaven,
and do not return to it
   without watering the earth
and making it bud and flourish,
   so that it yields seed for the sower and bread for
     the eater,
so is my word that goes out from my mouth:
   It will not return to me empty,
but will accomplish what I desire
   and achieve the purpose for which I sent it,"
     declares the LORD.

Isaiah 55:10–11

SECURITY

The grass withers and the flowers fall,
   but the word of our God stands forever.

Isaiah 40:8

Let all who take refuge in you be glad;
   let them ever sing for joy.
Spread your protection over them, O LORD,
   that those who love your name may rejoice
      in you.

Psalm 5:11

Reflections on
SECURITY

_____

_____

_____

_____

_____

_____

_____

_____

_____

_____

_____

_____

_____

_____

_____

STRENGTH

The LORD is the everlasting God,
    the Creator of the ends of the earth.
He will not grow tired or weary,
    and his understanding no one can fathom.
He gives strength to the weary
    and increases the power of the weak.
Even youths grow tired and weary,
    and young men stumble and fall;
but those who hope in the LORD
    will renew their strength.
They will soar on wings like eagles;
    they will run and not grow weary,
    they will walk and not be faint.

Isaiah 40:28–31

The LORD gives strength to his people;
    the LORD blesses his people with peace.

Psalm 29:11

STRENGTH

It is God who arms me with strength
 and makes my way perfect.
He makes my feet like the feet of a deer;
 he enables me to stand on the heights.
He trains my hands for battle;
 my arms can bend a bow of bronze.
You give me your shield of victory,
 and your right hand sustains me;
 you stoop down to make me great.
You broaden the path beneath me,
 so that my ankles do not turn.

Psalm 18:32–36

The LORD is the strength of his people,
 a fortress of salvation for his anointed one.

Psalm 28:8

STRENGTH

God will keep you strong to the end, so that
you will be blameless on the day of our Lord
Jesus Christ.

1 Corinthians 1:8

The plans of the LORD stand firm forever,
   the purposes of his heart through all generations.

Psalm 33:11

Though we live in the world, we do not wage war
as the world does. The weapons we fight with are
not the weapons of the world. On the contrary,
they have divine power to demolish strongholds.
We demolish arguments and every pretension that
sets itself up against the knowledge of God, and
we take captive every thought to make it obedient
to Christ.

2 Corinthians 10:3–5

STRENGTH

God's divine power has given us everything
we need for life and godliness through our
knowledge of him who called us by his own
glory and goodness.

2 Peter 1:3

Who shall separate us from the love of Christ?
Shall trouble or hardship or persecution or famine
or nakedness or danger or sword? ... In all these
things we are more than conquerors through him
who loved us.

Romans 8:35, 37

The joy of the LORD is your strength.

Nehemiah 8:10

In repentance and rest is your salvation,
    in quietness and trust is your strength.

Isaiah 30:15

STRENGTH

Jesus said, "My grace is sufficient for you, for my power is made perfect in weakness." Therefore I will boast all the more gladly about my weaknesses, so that Christ's power may rest on me. That is why, for Christ's sake, I delight in weaknesses, in insults, in hardships, in persecutions, in difficulties. For when I am weak, then I am strong.

2 Corinthians 12:9–10

I can do everything through Christ who gives me strength.

Philippians 4:13

In Christ all the fullness of the Deity lives in bodily form, and you have been given fullness in Christ, who is the head over every power and authority.

Colossians 2:9–10

STRENGTH

Thanks be to God! He gives us the victory
through our Lord Jesus Christ.

1 Corinthians 15:57

In your hands, O LORD, are strength and power
to exalt and give strength to all.

1 Chronicles 29:12

My flesh and my heart may fail,
but God is the strength of my heart
and my portion forever.

Psalm 73:26

STRENGTH

The eyes of the LORD range throughout the earth
to strengthen those whose hearts are fully
committed to him.

2 Chronicles 16:9

Your strength will equal your days.

Deuteronomy 33:25

**O my Strength, I watch for you;
    you, O God, are my fortress, my loving God.**

Psalm 59:9–10

Reflections on
STRENGTH

_____

_____

_____

_____

_____

_____

_____

_____

_____

_____

_____

_____

_____

_____

_____

TRUST

Trust in the LORD with all your heart
    and lean not on your own understanding;
in all your ways acknowledge him,
    and he will make your paths straight.

Proverbs 3:5–6

Commit your way to the LORD;
    trust in him and he will do this:
He will make your righteousness shine like
        the dawn,
    the justice of your cause like the noonday sun.

Psalm 37:5–6

With God all things are possible.

Matthew 19:26

Those who know your name will trust in you,
    for you, LORD, have never forsaken those who
        seek you.

Psalm 9:10

TRUST

Jesus said, "I tell you the truth, if you have faith as small as a mustard seed, you can say to this mountain, 'Move from here to there' and it will move. Nothing will be impossible for you."

Matthew 17:20

Now I know that the LORD saves his anointed;
　　he answers him from his holy heaven
　　with the saving power of his right hand.
Some trust in chariots and some in horses,
　　but we trust in the name of the LORD our God.
They are brought to their knees and fall,
　　but we rise up and stand firm.

Psalm 20:6–8

The LORD is my strength and my shield;
　　my heart trusts in him, and I am helped.
My heart leaps for joy
　　and I will give thanks to him in song.

Psalm 28:7

TRUST

You, O God, are enthroned as the Holy One;
    you are the praise of Israel.
In you our fathers put their trust;
    they trusted and you delivered them.
They cried to you and were saved;
    in you they trusted and were not disappointed.

Psalm 22:3–5

The LORD's unfailing love
    surrounds the man who trusts in him.

Psalm 32:10

O Sovereign LORD, you are God!
    Your words are trustworthy.

2 Samuel 7:28

I trust in God's unfailing love
    for ever and ever.

Psalm 52:8

TRUST

Trust in the LORD at all times, O people;
    pour out your hearts to him,
    for God is our refuge.

Psalm 62:8

O LORD, you will keep in perfect peace
    him whose mind is steadfast,
    because he trusts in you.

Isaiah 26:3

Fear of man will prove to be a snare,
    but whoever trusts in the LORD is kept safe.

Proverbs 29:25

God is not a man, that he should lie,
    nor a son of man, that he should change
        his mind.
Does he speak and then not act?
    Does he promise and not fulfill?

Numbers 23:19

TRUST

I know whom I have believed, and am convinced
that God is able to guard what I have entrusted to
him for that day.

2 Timothy 1:12

The LORD is good,
 a refuge in times of trouble.
He cares for those who trust in him.

Nahum 1:7

Guard my life, for I am devoted to you.
 You are my God; save your servant who
  trusts in you.

Psalm 6:2

Reflections on
TRUST

_____

_____

_____

_____

_____

_____

_____

_____

_____

_____

_____

_____

_____

_____

_____

_____

_____

UNITY

It was he who gave some to be apostles, some to be prophets, some to be evangelists, and some to be pastors and teachers, to prepare God's people for works of service, so that the body of Christ may be built up until we all reach unity in the faith and in the knowledge of the Son of God and become mature, attaining to the whole measure of the fullness of Christ.

Ephesians 4:11–13

We were ... buried with Christ through baptism into death in order that, just as Christ was raised from the dead through the glory of the Father, we too may live a new life. If we have been united with him like this in his death, we will certainly also be united with him in his resurrection.

Romans 6:4–5

UNITY

Jesus prayed, "My prayer is not for [my disciples]
alone. I pray also for those who will believe in me
through their message, that all of them may be
one, Father, just as you are in me and I am in you.
May they also be in us so that the world may
believe that you have sent me. I have given them
the glory that you gave me, that they may be one
as we are one: I in them and you in me. May they
be brought to complete unity to let the world
know that you sent me and have loved them even
as you have loved me."

John 17:20–23

How good and pleasant it is
　　when brothers live together in unity! ...
For there the LORD bestows his blessing,
　　even life forevermore.

Psalm 133:1, 3

UNITY

You are all one in Christ Jesus. If you belong to
Christ, then you are ... heirs according to the
promise. ... Because you are sons, God sent the
Spirit of his Son into our hearts, the Spirit who
calls out, *"Abba,* Father."

Galatians 3:28–29; 4:6

Just as each of us has one body with many
members, and these members do not all have the
same function, so in Christ we who are many
form one body, and each member belongs to all
the others. We have different gifts, according to
the grace given us.

Romans 12:4–6

**May the God who gives endurance and
encouragement give you a spirit of unity
among yourselves as you follow Christ Jesus, so
that with one heart and mouth you may glorify
the God and Father of our Lord Jesus Christ.**

                    Romans 15:5–6

Reflections on
UNITY

_____

_____

_____

_____

_____

_____

_____

_____

_____

_____

_____

_____

_____

_____

_____

_____

_____

_____

_____

_____

WISDOM

Blessed is the man who finds wisdom,
    the man who gains understanding,
for she is more profitable than silver
    and yields better returns than gold.
She is more precious than rubies;
    nothing you desire can compare with her.
Long life is in her right hand;
    in her left hand are riches and honor.
Her ways are pleasant ways,
    and all her paths are peace.
She is a tree of life to those who embrace her;
    those who lay hold of her will be blessed.

Proverbs 3:13–18

If any of you lacks wisdom, he should ask God,
who gives generously to all without finding fault,
and it will be given to him.

James 1:5

WISDOM

The statutes of the LORD are trustworthy,
　　making wise the simple. ...
The commands of the LORD are radiant,
　　giving light to the eyes.

Psalm 19:7–8

This is what the LORD says, he who made the
earth, the LORD who formed it and established
it—the LORD is his name: "Call to me and I will
answer you and tell you great and unsearchable
things you do not know."

Jeremiah 33:2–3

Surely you desire truth in the inner parts,
　　　　O LORD;
　　you teach me wisdom in the inmost place.

Psalm 51:6

WISDOM

The fear of the LORD is the beginning of wisdom,
  and knowledge of the Holy One is
    understanding.
For through wisdom your days will be many,
  and years will be added to your life.
If you are wise, your wisdom will reward you.

Proverbs 9:10–12

By wisdom a house is built,
  and through understanding it is established;
through knowledge its rooms are filled
  with rare and beautiful treasures.

Proverbs 24:3–4

The wisdom that comes from heaven is first
of all pure; then peace-loving, considerate,
submissive, full of mercy and good fruit,
impartial and sincere.

James 3:17

WISDOM

If you call out for insight
    and cry aloud for understanding,
and if you look for it as for silver
    and search for it as for hidden treasure,
then you will understand the fear of the LORD
    and find the knowledge of God.
For the LORD gives wisdom,
    and from his mouth come knowledge and
        understanding.
He holds victory in store for the upright,
    he is a shield to those whose walk is blameless,
for he guards the course of the just
    and protects the way of his faithful ones.
Then you will understand what is right and just
    and fair—every good path.
For wisdom will enter your heart,
    and knowledge will be pleasant to your soul.
Discretion will protect you,
    and understanding will guard you.

Proverbs 2:3–11

WISDOM

Wisdom is supreme; therefore get wisdom.
Though it cost all you have, get understanding.
Esteem her, and she will exalt you;
embrace her, and she will honor you.
She will set a garland of grace on your head
and present you with a crown of splendor.

Proverbs 4:7–9

The unfolding of your words gives light, O LORD;
it gives understanding to the simple.

Psalm 119:130

Whoever gives heed to instruction prospers.

Proverbs 16:20

To the man who pleases him, God gives wisdom,
knowledge and happiness.

Ecclesiastes 2:26

WISDOM

Wisdom, like an inheritance, is a good thing
    and benefits those who see the sun.

Ecclesiastes 7:11

How much better to get wisdom than gold,
    to choose understanding rather than silver!

Proverbs 16:16

The Spirit searches all things, even the deep things
of God. For who among men knows the thoughts
of a man except the man's spirit within him? In
the same way no one knows the thoughts of God
except the Spirit of God. We have not received the
spirit of the world but the Spirit who is from God,
that we may understand what God has freely
given us.

1 Corinthians 2:10–12

WISDOM

Those who are wise will shine like the brightness
of the heavens, and those who lead many to
righteousness, like the stars for ever and ever.

Daniel 12:3

Wisdom is sweet to your soul;
   if you find it, there is a future hope for you,
   and your hope will not be cut off.

Proverbs 24:14

He who gets wisdom loves his own soul;
   he who cherishes understanding prospers.

Proverbs 19:8

WISDOM

I, wisdom, dwell together with prudence;
  I possess knowledge and discretion....
Blessed is the man who listens to me,
  watching daily at my doors,
  waiting at my doorway.
For whoever finds me finds life
  and receives favor from the LORD.

Proverbs 8:12, 34–35

The path of life leads upward for the wise.

Proverbs 15:24

The holy Scriptures ... are able to make you wise
for salvation through faith in Christ Jesus.

2 Timothy 3:15

WISDOM

Do not forsake wisdom, and she will protect you;
love her, and she will watch over you.

Proverbs 4:6

The knowledge of the secrets of the kingdom of
heaven has been given to you.

Matthew 13:11

**I keep asking that the God of our Lord Jesus
Christ, the glorious Father, may give you the
Spirit of wisdom and revelation, so that you
may know him better.**

Ephesians 1:17

Reflections on
WISDOM

_____

_____

_____

_____

_____

_____

_____

_____

_____

_____

_____

_____

_____

_____

_____

_____

WORK

Commit to the LORD whatever you do,
  and your plans will succeed.

Proverbs 16:3

Nothing is better for a man under the sun than
to eat and drink and be glad. Then joy will
accompany him in his work all the days of the
life God has given him under the sun.

Ecclesiastes 8:15

Whatever you do, work at it with all your heart,
as working for the Lord, not for men, since you
know that you will receive an inheritance from
the Lord as a reward. It is the Lord Christ you are
serving.

Colossians 3:23–24

WORK

Serve wholeheartedly, as if you were serving the Lord, not men, because you know that the Lord will reward everyone for whatever good he does.

Ephesians 6:7–8

God is able to make all grace abound to you, so that in all things at all times, having all that you need, you will abound in every good work.

2 Corinthians 9:8

God will not forget your work and the love you have shown him as you have helped his people and continue to help them.

Hebrews 6:10

The man who plants and the man who waters have one purpose, and each will be rewarded according to his own labor. For we are God's fellow workers.

1 Corinthians 3:8–9

WORK

It was God who gave some to be apostles, some to be prophets, some to be evangelists, and some to be pastors and teachers, to prepare God's people for works of service, so that the body of Christ may be built up until we all reach unity in the faith and in the knowledge of the Son of God and become mature, attaining to the whole measure of the fullness of Christ.

Ephesians 4:11–13

In a large house there are articles not only of gold and silver, but also of wood and clay; some are for noble purposes and some for ignoble. If a man cleanses himself from the latter, he will be an instrument for noble purposes, made holy, useful to the Master and prepared to do any good work.

2 Timothy 2:20–21

Diligent hands bring wealth.

Proverbs 10:4

WORK

The wages of the righteous bring them life.

Proverbs 10:16

Diligent hands will rule.

Proverbs 12:24

Do you see a man skilled in his work?
  He will serve before kings.

Proverbs 22:29

Speaking the truth in love, we will in all things
grow up into him who is the Head, that is, Christ.
From him the whole body, joined and held
together by every supporting ligament, grows and
builds itself up in love, as each part does its work.

Ephesians 4:15–16

WORK

All Scripture is God-breathed and is useful for teaching, rebuking, correcting and training in righteousness, so that the man of God may be thoroughly equipped for every good work.

2 Timothy 3:16–17

All hard work brings a profit.

Proverbs 14:23

**May the favor of the Lord our God rest
        upon us;
    establish the work of our hands for us—
    yes, establish the work of our hands.**

Psalm 90:17

Reflections on
WORK

WORRY

Jesus said, "Who of you by worrying can add a
single hour to his life? Since you cannot do this
very little thing, why do you worry about the rest?
Consider how the lilies grow. They do not labor
or spin. Yet I tell you, not even Solomon in all his
splendor was dressed like one of these. If that is
how God clothes the grass of the field, which is
here today, and tomorrow is thrown into the fire,
how much more will he clothe you! ... And do not
set your heart on what you will eat or drink; do
not worry about it. For ... your Father knows that
you need them. But seek his kingdom, and these
things will be given to you as well."

Luke 12:25–31

WORRY

Blessed is the man who trusts in the LORD,
    whose confidence is in him.
He will be like a tree planted by the water
    that sends out its roots by the stream.
It does not fear when heat comes;
    its leaves are always green.
It has no worries in a year of drought
    and never fails to bear fruit.

Jeremiah 17:7–8

Jesus said, "Are not two sparrows sold for a penny?
Yet not one of them will fall to the ground apart
from the will of your Father. And even the very
hairs of your head are all numbered. So don't be
afraid; you are worth more than many sparrows."

Matthew 10:29–31

WORRY

Do not be anxious about anything, but in everything, by prayer and petition, with thanksgiving, present your requests to God. And the peace of God, which transcends all understanding, will guard your hearts and your minds in Christ Jesus.

Philippians 4:6–7

Cast all your anxiety on God because he cares for you.

1 Peter 5:7

In my distress I called to the LORD;
   I called out to my God.
From his temple he heard my voice;
   my cry came to his ears....
He reached down from on high and took hold
      of me;
   he drew me out of deep waters.

2 Samuel 22:7, 17

WORRY

The LORD is my shepherd, I shall not be in want.
    He makes me lie down in green pastures,
he leads me beside quiet waters,
    he restores my soul.
He guides me in paths of righteousness
    for his name's sake.
Even though I walk
    through the valley of the shadow of death,
I will fear no evil,
    for you are with me;
your rod and your staff,
    they comfort me.

You prepare a table before me
    in the presence of my enemies.
You anoint my head with oil;
    my cup overflows.
Surely goodness and love will follow me
    all the days of my life,
and I will dwell in the house of the LORD
    forever.

Psalm 23

WORRY

Do not fear, for I am with you;
  do not be dismayed, for I am your God.
I will strengthen you and help you;
  I will uphold you with my
    righteous right hand.

Isaiah 41:10

God will give relief to you who are troubled.

2 Thessalonians 1:7

Jesus said, "Do not let your hearts be troubled.
Trust in God; trust also in me. In my Father's
house are many rooms; if it were not so, I would
have told you. I am going there to prepare a place
for you. And if I go and prepare a place for you,
I will come back and take you to be with me that
you also may be where I am."

John 14:1–3

WORRY

Jesus said, "Peace I leave with you; my peace
I give you. I do not give to you as the world gives.
Do not let your hearts be troubled and do not
be afraid."

John 14:27

May the LORD **answer you when you are
      in distress;
    may the name of the God of Jacob
       protect you.
May he send you help from the sanctuary
    and grant you support from Zion....
May he give you the desire of your heart
    and make all your plans succeed.**

Psalm 20:1–2, 4

Reflections on
WORRY

_____

_____

_____

_____

_____

_____

_____

_____

_____

_____

_____

_____

_____

_____

_____

_____

_____

_____

_____

Look for these other Inspirio promise books
at your favorite bookstore:

*Promises for You from
the New International Version*

*Promises for Students from
the New International Version*

*Promises for Moms from
the New International Version*

*Daily Inspiration from
the New International Version*

*Daily Prayer from
the New International Version*